SANDWICH MAN

SANDWICH MAN

The Story of Urban Servant Allan Law

Jim Hoey

Jim Hoey

BEAVER'S POND PRESS

Beaver's Pond Press is committed to turning interesting people into independent authors. In that spirit, we are proud to offer this book to our readers; however, the story, the experiences, and the words are the author's alone.

Cover design by Paul Roff
Interior design and typesetting by Pat Maloney

ISBN 13: 978-1-64343-552-7
Library of Congress Catalog Number: 2024912654
Printed in the United States
First Edition 2024
28 27 26 25 24   5 4 3 2 1

Beaver's Pond Press
939 West Seventh Street
Saint Paul, MN 55102
BEAVER'S POND PRESS (952) 829-8818
www.BeaversPondPress.com

To order, visit www.itascabooks.com.

Contact the author at ajehoey@comcast.net for speaking engagements and interviews.

To those individuals and groups who provide for those in need, dedicated to helping the homeless, the disadvantaged, and the poor. May the good Lord bless you for your generous and selfless service.

CONTENTS

Chapter One

MEETING THE MAN

It is a gloomy midmorning on Saturday, April 15, 2017, and my good friend Bruce Hendrickson and I have just completed a carpet removal project in a South Minneapolis home he is about to sell as an agent for Edina Realty. In our separate vehicles, we are headed north on Hiawatha Avenue for the McDonald's located near Franklin Avenue on our way to peruse another property.

As a lifelong baseball aficionado, I am listening to the FM station KFAN and prospects for Paul Molitor's Minnesota Twins, wondering if the team could rebound from a disastrous 59–103 season. They will, of course, becoming the first MLB team to make the playoffs after losing one hundred games the previous year.

Driving past the 42nd Street intersection with downtown Minneapolis on the horizon, Bruce's 2002 Taurus takes a sudden right turn into McDonald's, and I follow him. *Did Bruce forget which one we were stopping at?* We park alongside each other and exit our cars. "Why are we at this McDonald's?" I query.

"Gotta see somebody here," he says as we strut toward the entrance. Bruce, one of those guys who goes about life with a perpetual smile on his face, reaches for the door and, with his big wide grin, tells me, "You are about to meet the most amazing man you have ever met in your life."

As he is telling me this, I observe a black Chrysler van parked twenty feet away. It has a lot of large white printing on the side of the vehicle. It is a riveting sight, and I stop to hold the door for myself and read a slogan splashed all over the driver's side that states, "Love One Another." I have no idea at this point what, if any, connection this has to the fascinating man I am about to meet. Certainly, the slogan is one I support, yet I am wondering what sort of wacko drives around with that sort of message on his ride.

We stride to the back of the restaurant, and Bruce thrusts his hand out to a long-haired and harried-looking older gentleman with a worn headband. Bruce says, "Jim, this is Allan Law."

I reach my hand out, and the guy with silver hair hanging down to his shoulders and a Sam Elliott–like mustache shakes it vigorously, saying with a cackle, "I am the craziest person you will ever meet, and you can call me Mr. Law."

We sit after ordering a few coffees, and my observational skills are dialed up to one hundred. Bruce acknowledges that he got to know Allan during his days as the hockey coach at Minnehaha Academy because Allan's nephew, Daniel, was a goaltender for the Redhawks, and Allan used to watch him play back in the 1980s. I quickly learn that Mr. Law was a Minnehaha grad, an alumnus of 1962. He regales us with a few stories about his thirty-two years as an elementary school teacher in the Minneapolis Public Schools. Bruce asks him if he slept any last night, and I ponder why he would say such a thing to him. Allan says, "I got a few minutes here and there in the van, but I think I'll catch a few winks before I go visit my dad."

Now I am really curious. What does a former teacher do in his retirement that makes an acquaintance ask if he got any sleep overnight? Mr. Law looks me in the eye with his steely gaze and says, "I told you I'm crazy."

Bruce says, "I'm sure you've seen stories about Allan and all he does to help the poor here in Minneapolis. He's a legend around here, and everybody knows him and what he does."

Allan says, "Yeah, a lot of people call me the Sandwich Man because I deliver sandwiches. I'm out in the streets all night, every night, from nine p.m. to usually ten the next morning. We get food to people and also try to get them clothes and bus tokens if they need them, whatever we can do to help the downtrodden."

I am stunned by what I am hearing. I'm truly awestruck by the level of commitment and sacrifice this fellow performs. He says he drives a black van with white lettering around to the places where he knows he will find people needing his benevolence. Yes, this is the man with the van parked outside, and now I am feeling like a jerk for wondering what kind of weirdo would drive around the Twin Cities with "Love One Another" adorned on the sides of his vehicle.

Mr. Law tells me he hasn't slept in a bed during nighttime hours in nearly twenty years. No, he's out on the streets, feeding, clothing, and helping the destitute all but two nights a year.

"All but two nights," I repeat.

"Yeah, I don't go out on Thanksgiving night and Christmas Eve, but otherwise I'm out there," Allan states. As Allan and Bruce banter back and forth, I am speechless, except for various times when I blurt out overtures of disbelief about the level of his selflessness.

After fifteen minutes of discussion about Mr. Law's life of service, I state, "Mr. Law, I need to write a book about you and what you are doing."

He pauses, and I expect excitement and appreciation for the offer. Instead, he says rather tersely, "This is not about me!"

I say, "Mr. Law, people need to know about what you are doing so they can be inspired to do whatever they can to be of service to people. Also, we can promote your organization's work and have a good portion of the proceeds of the sale of the book go to them. You are the conduit, and we will tell the story through you. It would be impossible to tell this story without you as the focal point."

It's clear he isn't enamored of this idea. Though it is obvious he is proud of what he is doing, he is not doing it for recognition, honor, riches, or fame. Bruce tells him that I have written five books and am working on others and that I am a man he can trust. I am wondering who the others in his organization are when he delivers another stunning revelation: his organization is basically him and one part-time assistant.

What? I am almost incredulous by now and can hardly believe my ears. I inquire, "You're telling me that you provide more than two thousand sandwiches per night and you have just one part-time employee?" Allan states that he has a yearly budget of $170,000 and estimates that he feeds thousands of people a year with the help of nearly ten thousand volunteers. *Come on!* I have never been more dumbfounded in my life.

Over the next five minutes, he gives me the general layout of his three-pronged program (Love One Another, Youth Builder Program, 363 Days Food Program), and Bruce laughs at me as he witnesses my jaw drop every ten seconds with yet another statistic or bit of information that shakes my world—in a good way, mind you. I have always loved words, especially adjectives, and I find all of them inadequate to describe what I am discovering.

After we have been visiting for an hour, the subject moves away from this servant savant and his amazing life. Bruce, Allan, and I start discussing political and economic issues, social and cultural events, sports, and religion—the gamut of the human experience. As stunned as I am by Allan's generosity and kindness to the less fortunate, I am mesmerized by his depth of knowledge about a myriad of topics. He's got an opinion about the new Tesla cars, and it sounds like he just left an engineers' meeting in Detroit. The US foreign policy initiatives in Syria and Israel: sure enough, Allan rips off a comment that would be worthy of any thirty-year veteran of the Foreign Service responsible for the Middle East.

Immigration, the unemployment rate, the state of political discourse, teenage fascination with technology, the learning styles of youngsters, the cost of private school tuition, racial concerns, recent inventions, cancer treatments, hairstyles, nutrition, the art of conversation, toothpaste favorites, good-looking women, et al. He is a talking Google. I inquire how he is so well-informed.

Law says, "I listen to the radio a lot." It is also apparent that he has strong opinions and isn't bashful about espousing them.

After an hour and a half, Bruce has to leave to see the next property, and Allan and I sit and converse for another hour. I have innumerous questions, and he has answers. I am enamored of his work and his quirky personality. I listen to his stream of consciousness. No doubt, this guy is a character in the true sense of the word. But a character, I learn quickly, with . . . true character.

Two hours before, I was told I was going to meet the most amazing person I had ever met. Bingo! Soon, we both have to leave McDonald's and, as we saunter toward the exit, I witness his Pied Piper routine. Three fellows who appear to be down on their luck call out to him, and he greets each of them by first name. As he asks about their lives, it's clear that they revere him. I give Allan my business card, and he says he will phone me later that afternoon.

On my way home, I am simply amazed by what just transpired. Is this Allan Law fellow for real? Apparently so. The guy is a real-life billboard of compassion, a true hero in a world racked with so much pain and sorrow. He's also a fascinating character to boot. My next thought is that if I do this book, my task will just be not to mess it up because this story will write itself.

Allan Law calls me four hours later and abruptly says, "What will I have to pay to do this book if we do this?"

I reply, "Nothing. We'll get the book done and get it published, and all the proceeds, or much of it, can go back to your foundation."

It is quiet on the other end, and he finally says, "Really?"

"Yes. I would be privileged to do this. It wasn't an accident or a coincidence that we met today, you know. It was divine intervention or perhaps divine intent. It was meant to be, and now it is my duty to do the best possible job getting your story of service out there. I will make sure everything written has your approval for accuracy purposes." I tell him that I reserve the right to make my own specific observations, however.

On the other end, a soft voice utters, "Okay."

After my conversation with Allan, I call Bruce Hendrickson and we have a long chat about the Sandwich Man. I tell him that his words were prophetic, that after just one meeting and one phone call, Allan could be the most amazing man I had ever met.

Hendrickson, who grew up in South Minneapolis and attended Roosevelt High, knows that territory well and is acutely aware of Allan's status there. "I have always considered him the Mother Teresa of Minneapolis," remarks Bruce. "He has done the work that nobody else has done and he has been a great resource for families to get social

*Allan Law (left) visits with Bruce Hendrickson at McDonald's
six years after the initial encounter with the author.*

services, especially in regard to housing and special assistance. He is considered a real hero, especially in the Black
community, because they trust him.

"If there is a need somewhere, Allan is there to help,"
adds Hendrickson, who recalls seeing him at hockey games
four decades ago. Hendrickson was the 1978–86 boys'
hockey coach and a physical education and health teacher
at Minnehaha Academy, a private school on West River
Parkway. Hendrickson and Law have a bevy of mutual
associations and connections with the Minnehaha community.

"Allan is a true character and certainly marches to the
beat of his own drum," continues Hendrickson. "But he has
always had great energy and a heart for those who don't
have a lot. Let's face it: How many people could work the
graveyard shift like he has done for all these years? No-

body else has done it. His biggest criticism over the years about the structured social services was that they weren't available late at night and into the early morning hours. He has filled that void.

"Imagine all the time and effort he has spent to accomplish what he has," says Hendrickson, who has had breakfast with Law sporadically over the years. "He has former students now in their sixties who still respect and revere him. While he can appear disorganized in many ways, he gets the job done. Allan has friends young and old all over the city."

In his housing pursuits, Bruce Hendrickson has often seen Allan's vehicle in parking lots around the city. "One time, I see his van and, as I get near the door, it's obvious he's sleeping. He wakes and tells me that he wanted to drive to his condo in Edina but was too tired and needed to get a few winks. I'll bet that happens all the time."

Within a week of a full year later, I call Mr. Law to tell him that I have a preliminary go-ahead to get started on the book from a noted publishing company and that we should proceed. On the night the Timberwolves clinch their first playoff appearance in fourteen years, Law calls me at ten p.m. to tell me that he is going to be out in Mendota Heights at Visitation School at two o'clock the next afternoon because a fifth-grade class is making sandwiches for him to disperse.

My friend Helen Wilkie, who works in communications at Visitation, helps me find the classroom. Before I get within forty feet of Steve Wright's classroom, the energy and passion of ten- and eleven-year-old youngsters is evident in the hallway. It is nearly two p.m., and when I enter the room, the assembly line is in full force and the kids' excitement and enthusiasm is clearly testing the usual boundaries.

One step after walking through the door, I am engulfed by the youngsters, who think that I am their conquering hero, Mr. Law. They withdraw like I have the plague when I explain that I am present to observe their volunteer work and to witness him in operation. One by one, they come up to introduce themselves with great fanfare and, of course, sticky palms. I am impressed by these twenty-four boys and girls with their cool twenty-first-century first names, and I quickly identify some real leaders. They are pumped yet respectful, and their sincerity for the project is genuine. It is a loud room, but the spirit of giving is paramount. It is readily apparent, also, that Mr. Wright is a true maestro as an educator and the kids respect him greatly.

Allan is running late, which is appreciated because the class needs ten more minutes to fill myriad loaves of Wonder Bread with bologna and cheese. (Kids, I did see some of that get gobbled up when you thought no one was looking!) The completed sandwiches are returned to the same plastic bread bags they came in and placed in plastic storage totes for shipment in Law's van.

Allan Law arrives twenty minutes late to Mr. Wright's classroom and is immediately besieged by the sandwich preparers. I will eventually learn that Allan lets life come to him, and time isn't always of the essence. The children have already witnessed a movie about his work entitled *The Starfish Throwers*, so they are well-versed in what Allan does. The documentary by Minneapolis filmmaker Jesse Roesler reviews the success of Love One Another, which was founded in 1967.

Mr. Law, who is now seventy-three, sits down in a chair toward the front of the room, and the kids gather around him in eager anticipation. I am seated next to ten-year-old Liam Edel, who is focused on his every word, just like the rest of his classmates. Allan, who is dressed in his customary flannel shirt, tells the kids that he spent four years teaching fifth grade. They cheer. No doubt he is comfortable in their midst. He's got a Mr. Rogers–like appeal.

As Law delineates his work for fifteen minutes, these Catholic schoolchildren listen and are quite impressed with not only his work but also his conversational style and easy demeanor. We all learn, and the kids are both amazed and amused at what he utters. He hasn't slept in a bed (at least at night) in over twenty years and never wears a coat or cap, even in winter. The kids turn to each other and shrug their shoulders. He goes to SuperAmerica (which will later be renamed Speedway) not to pick up doughnuts for himself but to pick up food for others. With each new revelation about his lifestyle, the children belt out a question and he responds.

Liam asks, "How does it make you feel to help people?"

Allan says, "It feels really good, just like when you help others. It's not healthy what I do, but I need to do it. Why do I spend all this time on the streets? Because the most important thing to me is believing in Jesus and helping people. It is my job to change lives; that's why I spend every night on the streets."

It is momentarily quiet as his thoughts burrow into their brains and hearts. Soon, hands are thrust into the air and eleven-year-old Phoebe Belfour is called upon. She asks a very practical question: "Why do you give out sandwiches?"

Allan answers, "Because they are easy to make and you can freeze them for a long time. Plus, it gets people like you involved in the process and makes you feel a part in helping others." The Sandwich Man explains that he stores them in the seventeen freezers he has at his Edina condominium. The kids laugh.

A youngster shouts, "How many sandwiches do you give out in a year?"

He replies, "Eight hundred thousand last year."

They shout out the number, almost in unison, hardly believing what they have just heard. Suddenly, the focus is on the homeless themselves. One child questions why there are so many people who have to live outside, especially in cold places like Minnesota.

Allan remarks, "It can be very complicated, but many of these homeless people have mental illness, and many have lost their jobs and have faced severe family problems. I feel so bad for them being without a home and means to support themselves, so I do what I can do. That means providing them with blankets, caps, gloves, coats, bus tokens, shoes—you name it. We gave out seven thousand pairs of socks in 2016. Unfortunately, the poverty just keeps getting worse."

Twenty sets of hands are still in the air when Mr. Law informs the class that he will have to load up the sandwiches in the van. Time for two more questions. A young lady wonders about his safety.

"No," he says, "I'm never fearful, but it is dangerous out there. I've only been robbed three times, and I hardly carry any cash, anyway."

The final question comes from a blond-haired lad. "How long are you going to be doing this?"

After a moment of reflection, Law remarks, "As long as I can." He thanks them for listening and for their willingness to help the cause, and they all clap enthusiastically.

Mr. Wright wraps up the visit with a heartfelt thank-you. Six youngsters from the class get the honor of loading the sandwiches into large storage bins and venture outside to Law's black van, where they are deposited. Photos are taken before the Sandwich Man departs. The students, all in their school uniforms, return to class with a skip in their step. They will all remember this activity and visit for a long, long time. I have spent decades in a classroom as both a student and teacher, but I don't know that I've ever witnessed such an emotional and dramatic scene as that afternoon at Visitation.

A few months later, on July 25, 2017, I arrive at VFW Post 555 on Lyndale Avenue in Richfield to speak to the Business Forum, which traces its founding to a luncheon meeting at the "Old Nicollet" Hotel in 1872. The organization was involved in civic affairs in Minneapolis and its environs and even initiated the movement that saw the establishment of the School of Business Administration at the University of Minnesota. At a previous speaking engagement, I had prepared commentary about my previous books (*Minnesota Twins Trivia, Puck Heaven, Minnesota Vikings Trivia,* and *Ike: Minnesota Hockey Icon*).

Bruce Crosby, a scintillating man who has scheduled me for the speaking role, is eating his lunch alone when I march into the room with my little cart with placards and some books. I reintroduce myself and tell him I am glad to be here to speak about my most recent book, *Honoring Those Who Honor*, a publication about the Fort Snelling Memorial Rifle Squad.

He looks perplexed while perusing my materials and says, "Are you here to replace the speaker today?" I tell him that we had agreed for me to speak about the rifle squad on July 25 at noon and show him my notes about the booking. He laughs and says, "I couldn't have made a mistake, could I?" Crosby checks his papers and says, "Sure enough, I double-booked you. So sorry." He tells me that I am welcome to have lunch with them and listen to the speaker.

I happily agree and ask, "Who is the speaker today, anyway?"

He bellows, "Allan Law. Ever heard of him? He's spoken here before."

I shake my head in amusement and respond, "He's the subject of my next book!" We both share a hearty laugh. No coincidence, just divine intention once again.

Bruce and I banter about Law, what an interesting guy he is, and what an incredible life he has lived. As members of the Business Forum began to assemble, I tell him that I would be glad to do a short introduction of Allan. With everyone gathered by noon, we sit and order from the menu. By 12:20, most of the food has arrived, and I eat quickly. When Allan arrives at 12:30, Crosby explains the situation and tells the crowd that I will speak for fifteen minutes about Allan while Mr. Law eats his meal. It's fun to speak off the cuff about Allan and his work, and many in the assemblage are already aware of his plaudits. After what appeared to be a successful talk, I introduce Allan to speak and leave the lectern. Allan, who has just received his steak sandwich, doesn't stand up but instead begins to speak while eating his lunch. I am surprised but also amused. Mr. Law is not a man of pretense.

I switch into the role of research reporter as Allan commiserates with the small gathering. He puts all of them at ease with his playful banter and one-liners, notwithstanding his unique ability to follow up an inquiry with a few other questions of his own and disparate commentary about anything that is on his mind. After a few minutes, he begins one-on-one interviews with the club members and finds a connection to every one of them. Didn't your uncle own a Sinclair gas station at 44th Avenue and 36th Street? Was your dad the guy who almost made the Olympics in speedskating in the 1960s? Wasn't your brother the assistant principal at Howe Elementary School? Allan's penchant for finding the associations is startling and impressive and has me shaking my head several times. The Forum members are all enamored of Allan and his unconventional style.

This being just my third time in his presence, I am learning much about his story and his ambitious program for the needy. His talk, although fascinating, is difficult to track, as he is all over the place. First, a story about a mechanic he knows from Bloomington Avenue. Next comes a tale about summer trips with students in the 1960s and . . . he also dished out thirty thousand toothbrushes . . . and in the next breath, he mentions his grandfathers both being alcoholics and that he has never had a drink in his life. Allan tells the listeners that he never asks for money for his organization when he speaks to groups, and they nod. Next, he says that he has never done any fundraising. The audience raises their eyebrows in unison. Law says he does send out an electronic newsletter each year, updating patrons and bene-factors on the status of his organization.

There are short pauses, of course, because Law has to take a bite out of his sandwich or smack down some more mashed potatoes. He has the audience eating out of his hand. The look on their faces gives it away. More than once, I have to quiet my giggling from witnessing this show. Allan has an easygoing persona; he's definitely an iconoclast, a real unique character, smart as a whip, outspoken, and a bit eccentric. Ever-present, however, is his sincere desire to help those who are in need. His Henny Youngman–style quips and retorts belie his caring nature.

His talk, which is sometimes a rambling dissertation on today's societal ills, is thought-provoking and audience-based. He takes on questions readily and remarks candidly yet defiantly, "I haven't read a book since I was in college." Really! Allan relays that he's conservative and cares not for so-called "political correctness" and that he just "tells it like it is." Nobody would need to be told this.

Allan Law states that his father, Loren, is 101 years old and lives in the same Edina condo where he owns a unit. Ears perk up as the younger Law says he has never slept there, seeing that in that apartment he has seventeen freezers filled with sandwiches he will deliver in the next month. Usually, he catches a few winks when and where he can. Amazing. This guy is seventy-three years old and he spends every night until the following morning on the streets, searching for people to help. It is at this point that it dawns on me that this fellow spends twelve hours on the streets and then doesn't crash to regain his energy and strength. He spends the daylight hours prepping for the next night.

What does he do after those exhausting hours? Well, he speaks to groups like the Business Forum, or he ventures to schools and churches to pick up more food and clothing with his van and then brings them to one of his twelve storage units spread throughout the metro area. I am lost in space for a few minutes as I calculate the gravity and substance of this self-sacrifice. It boggles the mind. Who can do this and stay healthy and sane?

I am brought back to reality when someone asks, "Are you ever concerned for your safety?"

Allan says, "No, the homeless trust me, and they know

what I do for them. It's crazy out there, no doubt." That's his go-to line, either speaking of the dire need these days or describing the gravity of his dedication. Allan Law says, "I'm crazy," at least ten times during his diatribe. "I don't hate anyone out there, but I sure hate what is happening out there," he adds. "I do what I think I should do, but the poverty is so much worse than when I first started doing this work in 1967."

At this point, his flip phone rings and he excuses himself to answer it. We listen to a Bob Newhart–like phone call from someone who requires help, and he tells the caller he will tend to the issue in an hour. When he returns after a minute, Allan doesn't miss a beat, regaling the members with a humorous yet telling story about race relations in the 1960s.

It is the summer of 1969, and Allan is piloting a Ford station wagon with seventeen Black children (all boys) aboard. He had started his 501(c)(3) nonprofit, Minneapolis Recreation Development, two years earlier, and it is time for a weeklong vacation to the Rocky Mountains for the inner-city kids. The program, he stresses, does not have any relationship with the city. The kids, aged eight to fourteen, aren't belted in, as most vehicles aren't required to have them equipped at that juncture. It's hot and there is no air conditioning. Imagine that scene as they cruise through southeastern South Dakota.

The Twin Cities contingent pulls up to a modest motel in a small town off the newly constructed freeway (I-90). The kids, of course, have plenty of pent-up energy and are dying to get out of the vehicle, and they're as hungry as wolves. Not yet. Law makes it clear that they are to stay in the car until he exits the motel office with the keys to the two rooms they will rent. They are adamant about getting out, but Allan is firm. They pout but agree to his request, telling him to hurry it up.

The motel is not a national chain but a local mom-and-pop operation with about twelve units. Allan saunters out into the hundred-degree heat and enters the tiny office, where he is greeted by a sweet, slender older woman. She is the proprietor and says that she has two rooms available, which is lucky as it is now late afternoon. Allan engages in small talk with the woman and forks over the forty-nine dollars for the two rooms. As the woman heads out with Allan toward the rooms, the kids rocket out of the Ford wagon toward them, startling the woman as they scream and yell in excitement.

As Law tells it, the lady shouts, "Hey, mister, do you know that you have a bunch of Black kids in your car?"

With a straight face, Allan calmly replies, "I never noticed."

The audience at the Richfield VFW that day roars and roars some more. It takes about a minute to subside. To be sure, it wasn't just a witty response. There is no racism in Allan Law. I truly believe, after getting to know him, that he doesn't see any color in people. They are just people. Indeed, many of the disadvantaged and unfortunate people he serves are Black or Native American, and he rarely mentions that part of the issue.

A query from the audience asks about his employees. He chortles and states, "We don't really have employees, per se, and we don't pay any salaries. I don't take a salary. I have my teacher pension. We have one part-time guy who runs our website and deals with our donations." It is quiet, and we are all shocked by that statement. It can't be true. Allan explains that the nonprofit relies on donations of money, clothing, food, et cetera. All the donations, 100 percent of them, go toward the work of Love One Another.

While we are contemplating that fact, Law informs the gathering that he operates this organization with his flip phone. He doesn't text, doesn't use email, and doesn't use a computer. This man tells us, "I am not a good businessman and don't care about that aspect of the business. My job is to go out and speak to volunteer groups that make sandwiches for us or want to donate clothing or whatever, and I collect the stuff and then store it. At night, I take my van and deliver whatever the homeless need, be it bus tokens, grocery cards, energy kits, toiletries, blankets, winter clothes, socks and shoes, boots—you name it. We have 177 organizations that sponsor us."

Yet again, I am impressed by the simplicity of this operation and stupified by its breadth of service. In this age of technology, Allan Law operates this lifesaving outfit with a flip phone. Seriously! It is hard to fathom the lack of technical savvy of this urban saint and square it with the scope of his service to humanity. Yes, saint! In an age when we think highly of ourselves if we volunteer an hour or two a week, this guy volunteers an average of sixteen to eighteen hours

Bruce Crosby (left) and Law at Richfield VFW Post 555

a day or, more likely, many more. More on that calculus later!

On the phone for your job? Allan figures that he receives about two hundred calls a day and tries to answer most. I am furiously trying to jot down all my observations while attempting to write his words verbatim for the sake of accuracy. As I am in the midst of scrambling to keep track of it all, Allan wraps up his talk. A hearty ovation follows. Nearly every one of the attendees remains to thank him and ask him further questions about his life on the streets. He patiently and graciously deals with each of them. I am now fully convinced that I would be humbled to somehow do him and his story true justice. The Twin Cities, the state, the country, indeed, the whole world needs to know about what one person can do to help others.

Unfortunately, between my part-time work for Bruce and my other book projects, my work on the book on Law takes a lengthy hiatus. Of course, COVID-19 throws a monkey wrench into the whole process too. Another issue is my long-standing belief that in order to truly understand Allan's commitment, I must absolutely spend at least a few nights accompanying him on his nightly sojourns helping the homeless. Wouldn't the author need to witness his efforts in person?

Law repeatedly rebuffs my inquiries into such an arrangement, stating that it is just too dangerous out there. I'm not concerned about my safety and still feel it is critical to see firsthand what he does, both at night and throughout his next day. Eventually, I begin to more fully understand his reluctance to let me ride along for the sake of observation. Allan says, "When I have somebody with me, the people on the streets think something is up, and it's just not comfortable for me or them. I want to protect their dignity. I get to know some of them well, and many are embarrassed or ashamed of their plight. Even when we filmed the documentary, many didn't want their faces shown because there were warrants out for them."

Another issue is my inability to contact him. When too many messages are left in his phone mailbox, it becomes almost impossible to communicate with or interview him. One of the main reasons for a ride-along or two is the need for photographs I will require to illustrate his work on the streets. However, after viewing *The Starfish Throwers*, I contact director Jesse Roesler and receive his permission to take images from his outstanding documentary. Problem solved, full speed ahead.

While one could get frustrated dealing with Allan Law, one could never get angry at him because he is aways up to doing good. He is an upbeat and likeable fellow, a truly endearing man. You never quite know if he's serious or just putting you on. He's quirky and opinionated, but those opinions are always about how life can be made better for people. His eccentric nature belies a brilliant mind; he's a simple man with a simple mission—to help others. Law says he doesn't need the recognition and all the glory, yet deep down, he loves the attention because he thrives on interaction with other humans and he loves being a character. The man is justifiably proud of his program, and no one can deny his incredible impact on literally tens of thousands of people.

Tributes to Allan Law's efforts in helping others could fill an entire book on its own. The affirmative adjectives that are used to describe his actions and his own personal attributes would fill an old-fashioned dictionary. In all the interviews I conduct for this project, there is one constant: they all have a smile on their faces. A strong majority of those people are also shaking their heads at the same time, as if they are unsure how to most accurately put into words their admiration and respect for what he has accomplished and for his legacy. This author certainly concurs. After seven years of stops and starts, it is time to tell his story, and to inspire others to act and do good in this world.

Chapter Two

LOVE ONE ANOTHER ORGANIZATION

In 1967, while teaching elementary school in the Minneapolis Public School system, twenty-two-year-old Allan Law founded Love One Another as an organization independent of his responsibilities as an educator. His motivation for setting up his fledgling company was simple—to help people. Over the next fifty-seven years, Law's volunteerism spurred thousands of others to volunteer themselves to help the poor, the disadvantaged, and the homeless of the Twin Cities. On any given night, there are an estimated ten thousand homeless people in the metro area, including three thousand children under age seventeen.

After thirty-two years of teaching in Minneapolis, Law retired to work on a nightly basis to provide food, clothing, personal-care items, and on-the-street care and support. At least 363 nights of the year, Law drives his black Ford van around the Cities to feed and provide emergency assistance to those less fortunate.

The name of the organization, Love One Another, sets the tone for its purpose—to give hope to the thousands it serves each year. It has also motivated approximately eight thousand people to volunteer for Law's burgeoning pro-

The Sandwich Man cruising downtown Minneapolis.
(Courtesy of Jesse Roesler)

grams. Law's personal crusade to deal with homelessness and poverty has earned him the monicker *the Sandwich Man* throughout the Twin Cities area and the well-earned respect of the people he serves.

Operating on a budget of less than $170,000, with in-kind donations, the four programs of Love One Another—the 363 Days Food Program, Samaritans Outreach, Youth Builder, and the Scholarship Program—deliver over $1,700,000 in support annually to those in need. The 363 Days Food Program alone distributes up to eight hundred thousand sandwiches each year.

Love One Another is driven entirely by volunteers, and no salaries have or will ever be paid to anyone working for the organization. Amazingly, there are really only two people who directly work for the outfit—founder and executive director Allan Law and part-time administrative

*Lanny Law, Allan's younger brother, working on
the organization's website at his home.*

director Lanny Law, Allan's younger brother. The vans uti-
lized for accruing and delivering goods to the benefactors
have been donated by either local organizations or specific
individuals who wish to remain anonymous.

All donations generated by the parent organization are
used for general operating expenses or purchasing pro-
gram-specific items. No rent is paid for office rental. Both
Allan and Lanny work out of their own residences. Allan
Law has a condominium on York Avenue in Edina where
he maintains seventeen freezers to store sandwiches. There
are several twelve-by-thirty rental storage rooms used for

Allan Law being interviewed at one of his storage units.
(Courtesy of Jesse Roesler)

storing various products located throughout the Twin Cities area, mostly in the western suburbs.

There have been as many as twelve storage rooms at one time, and the exact number at any time depends on the surge of donated items. Law started renting storage units in the late 1980s as the needs increased and especially after he retired in 1999, when poverty increased. There are also ten other freezers located at volunteer drop sites throughout the Twin Cities.

The official name of the organization as a member of the Minnesota Council of Nonprofits is Minneapolis Recreation Development, Inc. The Love One Another name is simply a slogan or motto for the 501(c)(3) organization. Interestingly enough, the slogan was the suggestion of Law's mother, Arlene. Since its founding, Love One Another has had as its guiding principle a quote from former United States vice president and Minnesota senator Hubert Humphrey:

> *"The ultimate moral test of any government is the way it treats three groups of its citizens. First, those in the dawn of life—our children. Second, those in the shadows of life—our needy, our sick, our handicapped. Third, those in the twilight of life—our elderly."*

What began as an after-school, weekend, and summertime program for inner-city youth has grown and expanded in scope to include four core programs.

Youth Builder Program

The Youth Builder Program was founded by Allan Law in 1967 to provide inner-city youth with free after-school, weekend, and summertime recreational activities. Over the years, it evolved to also include personal development, educational, cultural, and community-service activities. The focus was on preparing youth for the transition to middle school and high school and providing opportunities for advanced-placement programming, college career exploration, and after-school tutoring. The Youth Builder Program currently provides over three hundred underprivileged children annually with backpacks filled with school supplies, school clothing, and funding for field trips. Over the past fifty-seven years, the Youth Builder Program has served over sixteen thousand at-risk inner-city youth, help-

Allan photographed with the Minneapolis Recreation Development kids with downtown Minneapolis in the background, circa 1980s.
(Courtesy of Allan Law)

ing them develop the foundational skills to achieve their full potential.

363 Days Food Program

When he retired from teaching in 1999, Allan Law decided to expand his community outreach efforts. Due to the rapid growth in the number of people living below the poverty level, he began feeding the homeless and families in need on a daily basis, and the 363 Days Food Program became the cornerstone of that work. Law was grateful that certain charities had special meals on two days for the homeless—Thanksgiving and Christmas. The homeless enjoyed those full-scale meals, but what about the remaining 363 days? Law was determined to provide some basic type of food every day of the year.

He initially received donated unsold bakery goods and

Allan with youngsters making sandwiches. (Courtesy of Jesse Roesler)

sandwiches from several stores and gas stations. In addition, some churches and organizations that were aware of Love One Another began to make and donate sandwiches.

As a result of an incredible outpouring of donor support, the 363 Days Food Program has received and distributed an average of more than six hundred thousand sandwiches annually to the homeless and hungry for the past ten years. Sandwiches are donated by over five hundred community groups, churches, schools, individuals, and companies. In total, each year more than eight thousand individual volunteers, ranging in age from four to ninety-seven years old, participate in sandwich-making events.

The sandwich-making volunteers usually are composed of schoolchildren and church youth groups. Perhaps two-thirds of all the sandwiches are made by kids under age sixteen, and Allan especially enjoys speaking to such groups when collecting their bounty. When a group decides they want to make sandwiches, they must complete a request on the organization's website (www.mrdinc.org) and sign up for an event. Love One Another then confirms a date, sends sandwich-making instructions, and places them on their calendar for a pickup/speaking time.

The sandwich-making groups run the gamut: Girl Scouts, Boy Scouts, hockey teams, baseball and softball teams, family reunions, children's sleepovers, birthday parties, anniversary parties, even wedding receptions. How do people hear about this phenomenon? It is "word of mouth on steroids"; people have a good time at the events and then want to get involved and talk to each other. Most years, there are over six hundred such group events. Thus, there is an average of two events per day, but sometimes there are as many as five or six, and Allan usually appears at all the largest ones.

The sandwiches can be frozen up to sixty days, but the organization tries to keep inventory at thirty days. There are seven drop sites (churches or businesses) where the sandwiches are stored in freezers, which Love One Another purchases. At events with fewer than five hundred sandwiches, a representative of the volunteer group drives to the drop site and brings the sandwiches to the contact person at the church or business. When the freezers are full, Allan or another volunteer comes to pick them up.

When it is a larger event, Allan will arrive to pick them up and thank the group while speaking to them for fifteen to twenty minutes. The sandwiches are placed in large

31

The Sandwich Man thawing sandwiches on his condo floor.
(Courtesy of Jesse Roesler)

plastic totes and transferred to Law's van. Allan will then bring them back to his Edina condominium freezers or to a large frozen drive-in warehouse in Newport that can hold an unlimited number of sandwiches.

Love One Another distributes an average of two thousand sandwiches per night to the homeless and hungry living on the streets. They receive help from twenty-one Twin Cities partner organizations that also serve the homeless and individuals and families in urgent need:

- Salvation Army / Harbor Light Safe Bay, Minneapolis
- Catholic Charities Higher Ground, Minneapolis
- Catholic Charities Higher Ground, St. Paul
- Union Gospel Mission, St. Paul
- Salvation Army, West 7th St., St. Paul

- Salvation Army, Payne Avenue, St. Paul
- Avivo, Minneapolis
- Good in the 'Hood, Bloomington
- Park Harbor Homeless Ministry, Minneapolis
- Shelf of Hope: Gethsemane Church, Minneapolis
- Waite House, Minneapolis
- Hope Recovery, King of Glory Church, Minneapolis
- Bread of Life Church, Minneapolis
- Franciscan Brothers of Peace, St. Paul
- St. Vincent de Paul Church, Twin Cities
- Sharing and Caring Hands, Minneapolis
- Hospitality House, Minneapolis
- Little Earth Community, Minneapolis
- Marie Sandvik Center, Minneapolis
- Urban Ventures, Minneapolis
- MAD DADS Program, Minneapolis

Samaritans Outreach Program

The Samaritans Outreach Program provides basic living necessities for the homeless, the poor, and underprivileged children and their families. Responding to several calls for help each day, Allan makes stops to deliver food, clothing, personal-care items, first-aid kits, and emergency funds. Some of the food items include water, sandwiches, fruit, bakery goods, and baby formula. As for clothing, the main products distributed are winter coats, hats, boots, socks, and gloves. Blankets and diapers are also commonly given out. In 2018, the program distributed fifteen hundred pairs of handmade wool mittens donated by volunteers from Mittens on a Mission.

He also provides referrals to agencies that help with housing, counseling, chemical dependency, job placement, financial aid, and health care. Temporary housing has become a critical need in the Twin Cities over the past several years because homeless shelters are over capacity on most nights, and affordable rental housing has become scarce. The Samaritans Outreach Program provides short-term funding for people in need of temporary housing, rent, and prescription co-payments.

The program also distributes bus tokens to people without transportation to get to job interviews or medical or counseling appointments. Riding the bus also provides safe refuge from the streets and a shelter from inclement weather.

Scholarship Program
In 2016, Love One Another launched a scholarship program. Over the years, Allan Law has seen numerous lives remarkably transformed from homelessness and poverty to self-sufficiency through education. His long-term goal for several years was for Love One Another to be able to help deserving people begin that journey. The new program is a scholarship fund focused on assisting homeless adults and underprivileged youth in beginning to pursue degrees at local community colleges and technical schools.

No doubt, Love One Another has a truly unique approach that has evolved entirely from the compassion, vision, and drive of founder Allan Law. Over its almost fifty-seven-year history, Law has led its transformation from a small inner-city youth program to an organization serving at-risk youth and the homeless community. It is astounding to consider how it has thrived, and with no one being paid a full-time salary!

While you are enjoying a late-night TV show or watching a movie in the comfort of your home, imagine the enigmatic Law and his one-man show driving on the dark streets, awaiting those in need. And when you rise for work or school the next morning, he will still be out there providing sandwiches, toiletries, jackets, or first-aid kits to the needy. When he's done by ten or eleven in the morning, he will go to a local fast-food restaurant and field phone calls from his partners to pick up food or clothing. Just maybe, he will catch a few winks in the van. But alas, he has a speaking engagement at a church or school, where he will probably also give a twenty-minute talk on his organization. His twelve-hour nightly travels around the inner cities are often followed up by ten to twelve hours of hustle to make sure he's ready for the next evening. It's literally a twenty-four-hour circle of love. How much can the human body take without sufficient rest and recovery? A lot, apparently.

It is unimaginable that anybody could fill the role that Allan Law fulfills. First, there is the incredibly deep chasm of motivation to help. Second, one would need to have the energy and strength to execute that motivation. Third, there is the vision to create this whole scenario in the first place. Oh, yeah, and he does all of this with his one great technological tool—a flip phone. In this day and age, it's like racing in the Daytona 500 with a Model T.

Much of my knowledge about Love One Another and the nuances of the operations of one Allan Law are gleaned from Steven Aase, a part-time volunteer from 2012 to 2020. A few months after my meeting Allan, Aase contacts me to tell me that he is willing to help with whatever I need to proceed with the book. Steven was an invaluable cog in the machinery of the organization during his tenure, handling emails, texts, phone calls, and volunteer arrangements, as well as dealing with all the donations and the website. His official title with the organization was Head of Operations or Marketing and Development Consultant.

Aase, a native of La Crosse, Wisconsin, is an erudite gentleman with superb organizational and marketing skills. After serving with Allan Law for nine years, Aase became an invaluable resource of information for this project. A University of Minnesota graduate with a degree in business administration (1976), Steven spent sixteen years working for Pillsbury in marketing research at various locations around the country before returning to Minnesota in 2001. He ran a business for the businessman Curt Carlson after his Pillsbury stint. He has held several consulting jobs and has spent the past fifteen years working as a jack-of-all-trades in the nonprofit world, including two years at Minnesota Teen Challenge.

Technically, Aase was not an employee but a contractor for Allan Law's company. Steven was working for Life Rebuilders, a Christian halfway house in Minneapolis that helped work-release prisoners reenter society. Aase remembers, "A friend of mine there said he had a friend"—Allan—"who could use some fundraising help. Allan and I met at a coffee shop in Edina and I asked him what he did, and after five minutes of listening to him, I told him I didn't believe him. I couldn't imagine that it was possible for him to deliver all these sandwiches and to do the work that he does, almost all by himself."

So it was arranged that the friend at Life Rebuilders would pay Steven Aase to aid Allan Law and his organization. Thus, the standard of "no salaries" was maintained. Aase spent a year and a half helping collect sandwiches (up to one thousand per day) and speaking to and thanking groups that volunteered.

Being well-versed in electronic marketing, Aase was a boon to Love One Another because Law literally hates technology. Aase says, "He doesn't know it or understand that aspect of life. We are so different—we're like Oscar and Felix—but we were still able to joke about things, and he has a great sense of humor. I was his organizer and his consultant. Though we were very good friends, I really didn't see him that much. But we were on the phone constantly."

Indeed. On a typical day, Aase would call Law to tell him where and when to pick up sandwiches. At many of those stops, of course, Law gave a talk about his program and thanked their partners. On occasion, when the need arose, Aase picked up sandwiches and spoke to groups. As there is no organizational office, Aase worked from home and out of his car. On occasion, he would meet Allan to

Steven Aase (left), Law (center), and a volunteer at a storage unit.
(Courtesy of Jesse Roesler)

bring him sandwiches or donated items or go directly to one of their twenty-one partners to deliver food or clothing.

Of course, those sandwiches have to be frozen and stored in one of his condominium freezers. That means that off yet another all-nighter, Law has to make daytime forays to various locations in the Twin Cities to gather them and return them to his residence. Donations of clothing and other necessities require a trip to store them in one of the storage areas scattered about the Twin Cities. Is it any wonder that Mr. Law has a difficult time being on time for scheduled appointments? Just know that he is up to good, despite weather or traffic conditions he can't control.

Asked about Law's greatest attributes, Aase responds, "Allan is remarkably good at listening and lessening tension in tough situations. He is totally selfless, and I think he got that from his mother. He's got a photographic memory to remember people's faces, their names, and something about them, and that is a remarkable trait. In addition, he may be the most compassionate person I have ever met and is empathetic to a fault.

"Allan is a very intelligent man, and he truly cares about others," continues Steven. "He has a tremendous amount of concern about everybody; it's just in his DNA. He's intuitive and he knows people, so he's nobody's fool. I've seen him and experienced his effect. Allan can be very stubborn and understanding to a point, but he wants people to help themselves; he always gives a lesson to them.

"Out on the streets, Allan encourages the homeless to be hopeful and to also try to help others by paying it forward. He really believes in the 'pay-it-forward' concept, in whatever small role they can do so. He tells the benefactors of the sandwiches what group made it for them so they are appreciative and thankful. It really personalizes the giving to the homeless.

"Allan Law has created a movement in the community where thousands of people have rallied around his message," says Steven. "The effort to help people is just amazing in its consistency and sustainability. He is a rolling vessel of compassion, and he's not a narcissist; he has no desire for hero worship."

Known for being reticent about others joining in his nightly drives among the homeless, Law has good reason for his "one-man-band" deliveries. Aase says, "Allan has only let a few people ride with him on his deliveries because he is firstly concerned about danger for his passengers. If he's alone, people trust him. If someone is with him, the homeless get uneasy. Homelessness is a transient thing, and he doesn't want to cause distress in them because of the pride they have. He is protecting them."

Aase, an Apple Valley resident, states, "I love Allan Law and the mission that he has undertaken and was honored to work for and be associated with the organization. My service ended when [Allan's] younger brother Lanny's son and daughter could take over my role, and that was fine with me. I absolutely loved representing Allan and promoting his laudatory efforts."

Indeed, there was a transition for the organization on March 1, 2021, when Law's niece, Christine Law-Chapman, became the manager of marketing and communications and his nephew Kevin Law began assisting with event logistics, picking up donated items from events and managing the storage rooms. Christine has a degree in human resource management and has broad experience with nonprofit organizations as a counselor, program coordinator, and consultant. Kevin has a degree in video digital arts and experience in supply chain management.

Love One Another is most certainly a bare-bones operation and purposefully so. It is efficient. Costs are minimal. Allan pays for his own health insurance. The vehicles driven by Allan are donated. The biggest expenses are the storage units that hold donated items, gas for delivering items, and maintenance on their vehicles. Accounting is easy because there is just one checking account for the organization. Allan never uses the company's checks for his personal use, either, and even pays his high electric bills at his condo with his own account. A CPA in Wayzata does stellar work for a reasonable price.

Lanny summarizes, "We are a fly-by-night outfit and prefer it in that manner. We exist to help people, and Allan is our one-man delivery man. The allure of our approach is that we are not bloated with big administrative or overhead costs. Others have told us that the simplicity of our operation is brilliant; we are unique in that we do not pay any salaries and have very low administrative costs. People that donate to us know where the money is going—to the people who need it. In addition, our volunteers get to participate in the process and that makes them feel good too."

Lanny checks the nonprofit's email ten times a day Monday through Friday, and he can get his daughter Christine to give technical help or get his son Kevin out to help with the storage units or with picking up sandwiches or other donations when required. He is in constant connection with his older brother to provide symmetry to the operation.

A few years ago, a dean of public affairs at a prominent West Coast university became familiar with the uncomplicated organization. He stated, "The head of the organization takes no salary and lives on his own retirement, the organization has no real employees and pays no salaries, and they take no money from the state or federal government. Is it a marvel why people want to donate and volunteer?"

It's a novel idea, no doubt. Thus, literally thousands of

people are inspired to participate in its mission and feel a part of it. These helpers cut across religious, racial, ethnic, and age lines to make sandwiches, knit and donate clothing, and even donate vehicles to be a cog in this machine of goodwill.

Lanny Law studied nonprofit management at the Humphrey School of Public Affairs at the University of Minnesota and completed that master's in public affairs program in 2017. He remarks, "I wanted to better help Allan's organization and be equipped to run it whenever he isn't able to. I want to carry on his philosophy and mission."

Allan Law has literally spent his entire adult life devoted to helping inner-city youth, families, and the homeless find hope via much-needed food and living necessities. He gives people dignity with his friendly disposition, inquisitive mind, and certainty that these people need kindness and understanding as much as they need food and comfort.

His service has given hope to thousands, and he is revered by those he serves and by the people who are in the business of serving others. His ease with people with serious problems is readily apparent, as a large portion of the homeless community suffers from mental and emotional issues. He is so cognizant of maintaining the dignity of the people that he serves that he is reluctant to have observers ride with him, as it was in my case.

The primary metrics used to measure the success of Love One Another are fiscal efficiency, volunteer participation, and the total number of homeless people they serve annually. As mentioned previously, the organization operates on an annual budget of less than $170,000 but delivers over $1,700,000 in support (with in-kind donations) annually to those in need. Metrics alone, however, cannot measure the appreciation of those served by Allan Law and his volunteer friends.

Chapter Three

COMMUNITY HELPER

A lthough Allan earned his nickname, the Sand-wich Man, for his late-night and early morning trips in search of the homeless over the past three decades or so, he was at work in the community more than fifty years ago. Instead of searching for the destitute and the downtrodden, Law was knocking on the doors where his students lived. It was something he would do for the entirety of his first career.

Starting in the fall of 1967, elementary school teacher Allan Law ended his day job as a fifth- and sixth-grade instructor in the Minneapolis Public Schools at around four p.m., but his day (and evening) was long from over. For the next thirty-two years, the former Minnehaha Academy High and University of Wisconsin-River Falls graduate would be spending his nights and weekends helping disadvantaged youth throughout Minneapolis. Most school nights (Sunday through Thursday), Law was working with youngsters from both North and South Minneapolis, bolstering their self-esteem and providing educational and entertainment opportunities for those who, for whatever reason, would not have had those experiences.

"As soon as I started teaching, I saw the situation so many kids were in," remarks Law. "It was a void I felt I was

44

Allan at the governor's mansion in St. Paul, circa 1980s. (Courtesy of the Law family)

destined to fill. Of course, there was a considerable problem with poverty, and so many were growing up without a father too. Plus, the neighborhoods many of them lived in provided the wrong kind of examples."

In 1967, Law established Minneapolis Recreation Development in order to provide fun activities and stability for those in dire circumstances. During those early years when the focus was on the children, Allan spent his own money on food and entertainment so that the impoverished kids had something to eat and activities to broaden their horizons.

"Man, we had a lot of fun in those days," remembers Law. "I would pick up the kids and we would do all sorts of activities, such as bringing them to the Capri Theater in North Minneapolis, to pro wrestling at the Minneapolis Armory, to Valleyfair and the stock car races in Shakopee, to

Twins games at Met Stadium and the Metrodome, to Gopher basketball games, and to the Mall of America and the State Fair. We took them for boat rides on area lakes and even for plane rides at Fleming Field in downtown St. Paul. And, of course, there were always trips to McDonald's."

People may wonder how a young white man was able to find trust in the Black community, enough for parents to allow this fellow to venture to local and regional venues with their offspring. Dennis Massie remembers it all so well. Now sixty-five, Massie was eleven years old in 1970 when Law was serving as a substitute teacher in his fifth-grade class at Sheridan Elementary in Northeast Minneapolis.

Not only was Law taking them out for entertainment and education, but he was also enlisting his students to sell candy in order to earn spending money and to help earn their own way, so to speak, to participate in all of his ventures. Massie lived on Washburn Avenue in North Minneapolis but was bused to school at Sheridan, which is located at 1201 University Avenue.

"Mr. Law shows up at our front door with a few neighborhood kids and asks my mother, who was single, if I could join them in selling candy," remembers Dennis. "Mom was very reluctant to let this man take me with him, as I didn't know he was a teacher until I had him as a substitute a little later on. I didn't get to go with him until my mother found out how sincere he was in trying to help us out and how trustworthy he was and how good he was with all the kids."

Massie, who has been on the Love One Another board

of directors for over ten years, says, "The word spread that this white man was for real, that he really did care and that his motivation was simply to help. After a while, we even forgot that he was white because he never saw race or color in people, he just saw people as people, not as white or Black or Native American or whatever.

"We sold candy every weekend for a couple of years," continues Massie, who now lives in Maple Grove and is married with three children. "Mr. Law brought us to different suburbs and cities like St. Cloud, Rochester, Red Wing, and Mankato, and we were exposed to different people and learned how to conduct ourselves as salesmen. He trained us so we represented ourselves well, and we learned a lot about being poised and how to handle ourselves."

Queried about what lasting things he learned from Law, Massie states, "First, it would be to be compassionate in loving others; second, it would be forgiveness, as we are called to do this, and I have seen him exhibit this and have never seen him really angry at someone for doing something stupid or wrong. Third, it would be perseverance, which is pretty self-explanatory with how he has lived his life. Lastly, it would be simplicity; just look how successful he has been with his bare-bones operation.

"Mr. Law knows how to be a 'schmoozer' and is kidding around and being lighthearted all the time," adds Massie, who graduated from Marshall-University High in Minneapolis in 1978. "He's still a very humorous guy, and I have seen him that way on the streets too. I also recall that he loved Elvis Presley because of his giving nature, his spirituality, and his positive relationship with the Black community."

Despite his compassionate and loving nature, Allan Law believes that even those undergoing homelessness are not off the hook. It's not simply 100 percent generosity going their way. He often tells the people he serves, "Try to do something good for someone, even if it is the smallest gesture, and think more about other people and not just yourself. Everybody can do something to better themselves." Mr. Law continues, "The most important thing I bring them is not sandwiches or clothing but . . . hope. Everybody needs it to live, and God will get you through things."

Law's life's work has inspired Massie to develop his own unique contribution to the poverty/homelessness conundrum. He established his own 501(c)(3) nonprofit, Massie's Mobile Mission, in 2021, and the company started its work on the streets in 2022. Dennis, the firm's president, designed his mission to go where there is a need. Thus, he purchased a high-top van with a large window that opens to the outside from Rudy Luther for a deep discount. In the program's infancy, the van would station itself outside the Salvation Army in Minneapolis or the Dorothy Day Residence in St. Paul from five thirty to nine p.m., but it now finds other locations too.

In the van, volunteers from the University of St. Thomas (two men and a woman) deliver food or supplies for the needy. Meanwhile, there is always a greeter to welcome those who may need help. Turkey, chicken, or bologna sandwiches—as well as water, apple juice, pop, chips,

Dennis Massie pictured with his van for Massie's Mobile Mission.
(Courtesy of Dennis Massie)

granola bars, popcorn, beef jerky, and other snacks—are served at the large side window. They also issue personal care items such as soap and shampoo that come from Allan Law's organization, which has also donated shoes and clothing.

"The idea to have a 'serving van' was planted on me on Allan's board, and he encouraged me to do it," says Dennis. "I am proud that I am serving in Mr. Law's legacy, and if it is successful, it will make me so happy. It has been very rewarding getting this going and the best way to give tribute and honor to Allan. The torch has been passed to me, and I have to do my part; I can't ever repay what he has done for me. I am serving the Lord, and that is a comfort. I think Mr. Law is real proud of me." Indeed.

Dennis Massie, an upbeat and dynamic man, relates two stories that Mr. Law told him recently that show insight into the reality of his life. In the first, in the middle of a bitter winter night, Allan confronts a desperate situation in a Satellite toilet in Minneapolis. He finds a woman and her boyfriend asleep. He rouses them and brings them to Hennepin County Hospital in his van. The woman has no feeling just about everywhere but ends up with frostbite only on her hands. Allan returns to the streets.

In the second story, Allan approaches a man who does not have any shoes. Allan, not surprisingly, gives his footwear to the unfortunate soul. He drives to the nearest Target store barefoot with his new friend in tow. Law is rebuffed at the store because of the "no shirt, no shoes, no service" policy that most stores employ. How ironic! Allan tries to convince the store employee about the peculiar situation but to no avail. Law rips a few twenty-dollar bills out of his wallet and gives it to his new friend, and the fellow heads in to buy a pair of new shoes. No word on whether or not the purchase turned out to be tennis shoes, slippers, or dress shoes!

"Here it is, now more than fifty years later, and he is still affecting my life," relates Dennis, who has worked for Costco in electronic sales for the past eleven years after operating his own limousine business for many years. "He's not just a friend or a mentor to me but a true father figure. I'm not the person I am today without Mr. Law. If I get in a spot, either personally or professionally, I call him because he's the guy. I usually call him at two a.m. because it's the only time I can reach him, if at all. If I have him on speed dial, then I am good. Who else would I want other than an angel like him?"

As for this book, Massie says, "I'm so glad we are getting the word out about his amazing story, a man who has given most of his life to truly help people. He is an incredible person and I trust him fully. He just loves people and never gives up on anyone, and I have witnessed that. There have been occasions when he has saved people's lives; even the police respect him because he gets involved in situations where they won't go. He's armed with Jesus Christ, and we know how powerful he is. Speaking about Mr. Law provokes great emotion in me."

Mr. Law lives in the "danger zone," according to Massie. He elaborates, "The places he goes are truly scary; when he is out there at night and in the wee hours, it can be life or death. I marvel at what he does and what he has accomplished, and I know I couldn't do it. When the riots broke out after the George Floyd situation, it didn't stop him. His great compassion and empathy for the less fortunate has definitely harmed his health, but he perseveres.

"However, whatever suffering Mr. Law has to undergo on this earth is only temporary," says an emphatic Massie, who also is buoyed by his strong Christian faith. "What he is earning, of course, is eternal life. He is driven to do this crazy, good stuff that he does for such a purpose. Yet he's out there, in pain, with all his bodily hurts, and he's doing it night after night. He's dog tired all the time, but he's still smiling and making silly jokes and making life just a little bit easier for thousands."

Massie's wife, Danielle, adds, "Allan had dedicated his whole life to helping people. Who else does that? Nobody, except for Allan. His motivation for doing what he does is based totally on a real true dedication to people."

Trace Massie, Dennis's younger brother, was also a student in Law's class and also serves on his board. Trace is now sixty-three years old and a resident of Inver Grove Heights and has been employed as a construction truck driver for nearly twenty years after running his own shipping business for eleven years. Trace was eight years old when he met Allan for the first time. He says, "My older brother Lloyd was in his neighborhood program before Dennis and I met him.

"Our neighborhood, roughly between 14th and 17th Avenues and between Thomas and Xerxes, had no boys' club or activities for youngsters," recalls Trace. "Allan got familiar with the parents to earn their trust so we could sell candy, and the program really grew. Our mom got very comfortable with him, so that wasn't a problem. All three of the Massie brothers would go all the time, and we were eight, nine, and ten years old at the time, and we had a blast. We hung out with the boys from the Grays family, and they always had money in their pockets selling candy under Allan, so we wanted part of the action."

Trace Massie has fond memories of traveling throughout the Twin Cities suburbs and the region on those weekends. Mr. Law always arranged for permits to sell the candy in each community, and the people were receptive and generous. Not only were the kids learning entrepreneurial skills, but they were making cash and also downing some candy too. Not a bad benefit for youngsters their age.

One summer day in nearby Brooklyn Center, the kids went door-to-door. Trace ambled up the sidewalk to a rambler and tried to open the screen door. It was locked. In the next instant, a large dog barreled through the screen and drove Trace down the steps. In the mayhem, Massie dropped the candy as he attempted to defend himself. The dog retreated as Trace was lying stunned on the sidewalk. Suddenly, the dog attacked again with a fury and bit his left arm. The owner came out to control the dog as Trace checked out his wound. His arm was bleeding but not profusely. Courageously, he even sold the dog's owner a few boxes of candy but, unfortunately, the owner didn't offer him any help for his wound.

Sure enough, Trace continued on with his planned route, but Law met up with him and inspected the injury. It was rather serious and would need care. They returned to the scene of the accident but, again, didn't get much help or concern from the owner. They reported the incident to the authorities, made a visit to a local clinic, and got treatment for the arm.

On another occasion, the Minneapolis contingent was selling in a certain town in southern Minnesota and, as it was, had a permit to sell. While Trace was calling on a home, a policeman walked up to him and told him and two others that he was not supposed to be selling candy. "He brought us to jail and actually placed all three of us in a cell," states Trace, still dismayed at the thought to this day.

"We waited until Mr. Law got there, but it was about an hour and that was not a good feeling at our age, let me tell you. It just didn't make sense to us, especially because we had our ID badges on with our name, our photos, and Minneapolis Recreation Development displayed on it.

"Wow, Mr. Law was pretty hot when he arrived, and we were so relieved, you can imagine," remarks Trace. "Allan was aghast that they put us in a cell, let alone bringing us to the jail. At the most, they should have left us in the lobby or the waiting area. It was maybe the only time I saw Allan get real riled up."

Trace Massie, a pleasant and genial sort, adds, "I am so proud to have known him and the spirit that he brings. I learned so much from him about discipline, especially in regard to presenting myself in public while selling candy. Despite that one incident, he taught us how to be cheerful in the worst conditions and how to see the good in every situation."

Asked about what makes Mr. Law unique, Trace says, "He focuses on your humanity, not on your condition or station in life. Most importantly, he tells you the truth. He used to get on our case if we needed straightening out. For impressionable youth, he set the stage for us to be successful and honorable young men. Even as a teenager, he would check up on us and see how we were doing and we did likewise. Allan could reach you at your level.

"The people who he has helped, they perceive him as a great asset to the community," Massie states. "He has seen the worst of the worst but he still stays positive. They love him, all the people who understand the depth of his contributions and who have witnessed his efforts. It's hard to miss his charisma, and he looks beyond race, gender, age, and ethnicity. To him, a person is a person and each has dignity."

In the summer of 1969, Minneapolis Recreation Development started traveling out of state in search of new destinations. Aboard the Love One Another six-passenger station wagon were Black youngsters. Law regrets, "The biggest frustration was that we had to limit our group to fifteen kids, and many who wanted to go weren't able to; plus, we brought just the boys at that time."

Trips were made in the 1970s and '80s, without air-conditioning, to places like the Black Hills of South Dakota, Yellowstone and Grand Teton National Parks in Wyoming, and Pikes Peak and the mountains of Colorado. "The kids got to see Mount Rushmore and the Crazy Horse monument, and seeing them ride go-karts in the Colorado mountains was wild. Of course, the kids had a stake in those trips, as they earned the spending money themselves, and that made them feel good about themselves. Certainly, those were very memorable trips for them and for me.

"We would cover about four thousand miles in ten days, and they piled up a lot of experiences in that time," says a smiling Law. "We even went to my grandparents' farm in North Dakota, and that was a wonderful new adventure for kids from the inner city to experience."

Chapter Four

OUT ON THE STREETS

It was the summer of 1999 and Allan was a recent retiree from the Minneapolis Public School system. The world was his oyster. Exotic vacations, world travel, golf outings, cruise excursions, and more beckoned. Not for this fellow. A second and possibly even more meaningful life was ahead.

"After retiring, now I could start spending the entire night on the streets," says Law. "Homelessness was already increasing back then, and many other nonprofit organizations were closed at that time, except the shelters. I eventually switched my focus to the inner cities of Minneapolis and St. Paul. I am proud that my organization has never received public funding for any of the items that have been given to the program; not from the city, the state of Minnesota, or the federal government."

Even during the COVID-19 crisis, he didn't apply for funds when state and federal governments were offering monies for nonprofit organizations. Love One Another purchases what is needed with the significant donations given by individuals, corporate organizations, and religious communities.

Once out on the streets, Mr. Law realized that there was a great need for services, especially after nine p.m.; in fact, he says that after one a.m., he is often alone out on the by-ways, and that includes the police. "I came to the conclusion that I needed to be helping through the night," states Law. "So I began staying out until midmorning, looking for people who were in dire need of blankets, socks, food, bus tokens, and personal care items." Law became the guy who was always bearing loads of sandwiches, thus the moniker, the Sandwich Man.

Speaking of bus tokens, Allan buys them a thousand at a time for one dollar or half-price and hands them out like candy during the winter months. He figures that he hands out at least two hundred a night and up to six hundred but usually not more than two or three per person. His yearly budget for bus tokens has reached as high as $75,000 per year.

As for socks, the homeless use them not only on their feet but also on their hands and even around their necks to keep warm. Energy packs, in small plastic bags, usually contain four items that the homeless can keep in their pockets and snack on during the cold nights; most typical are granola bars, chocolate bars, and packs of peanuts.

Danger constantly lurks, however. Despite his goodwill and constant presence on the streets, Law is more than aware of what may transpire with the ne'er-do-wells. Allan states, "Sure, many of the people out there in the wee hours know of my reputation, but not all of them do, and you never know about the gang element.

"I have never been close to the police," says a courageous Allan. "One time a cop said to me that I was doing wonders out here on the streets with all these knuckleheads and that I was crazy for going into places 'where we don't go unless we have two squads there.' I've had others in law enforcement tell me that some areas might be a little safer because of my presence there and that they hear my name mentioned a lot."

Despite all his years on the streets, Law is not immune to potential crime and violence. It is a concern voiced by nearly every group he speaks to. He proudly proclaims his familiar refrain, "I've only been robbed three times, and each time I didn't report it to the police; I just handled it myself. I just trust that God will protect me and don't really worry about it."

Perhaps it is wise that Law carries little cash on him on his nightly trips. On the most minor of the occasions, three young men with weapons in North Minneapolis attempted to rob him around two a.m.; however, one of the accosters knew Law, so they relented and let him go without further incident.

A few decades ago, at about one a.m., Allan heard from a lady he knew that her niece (around twelve or thirteen) was living in an apartment on the North Side, and she was concerned that there might be sexual impropriety involved. Allan drove up to the building, which was just a block from one of his former residences. He recalls, "I went into the back of the building and saw seven young men loitering around; I walk by them and head upstairs to her apartment. I knock on the door and there are four or five guys who are there but there is no sign of the girl."

They took his wallet and relieved him of two hundred
dollars (money he had been given by a friend that day because Allan was to buy paint the next day and paint his
apartment) and then one of the robbers said, "Let's just kill
him." Allan said a quick prayer. In relating the story, it almost sounds like a comedy. But it was real and Allan Law
is street smart. So what did he do? Allan's voice changed
and he started talking "street cred." While Allan was playing his animated role, one of the robbers said, "He doesn't
sound like he's white." Years later, Law says that's what
may have saved him. He does remember that two of the
fellows had guns and at least two had knives.

"Maybe it was the gangs I was mentioning and other
organizations that got their attention," says Law. "They
started talking among themselves and they didn't know
what to do with me. They were all high, for sure. They took
my keys and went out to my car. One guy came back and
threw the keys against the wall, saying all I had in the vehicle was food and toys."

The rest of the story strains credulity. Law thought about
running to the third-story balcony and jumping down to
the parking lot but instead made a dash for the keys and
scrambled out the door and down the stairs. The chase was
on, and a skirmish ensued in the hallway near the back
door in which Allan broke his middle finger. Law managed
to break free and he ran toward a nearby building where a
teacher friend lived. The pursuers gave up after a block or
so.

No, this saga isn't over just yet. Allan's teacher friend

gave him a ride back to the site of the crime early the next morning. His car was still there, but Allan had other ideas first. "It may have been real stupid of me, but I went back into the building to find my glasses and my wallet and, amazingly, I found them both and the credit cards were still there," recalls Law. "Then, I drove to Kmart in South Minneapolis to buy paint."

Law was in line to purchase the paint when he eyed one of the perpetrators from seven or eight hours ago. Allan says, "I wasn't scared and I started talking to him, but he played dumb like he didn't remember me. I told him that he didn't seem so brave now, and we got into a physical confrontation right there. I had taken some tae kwon do lessons so I used a few of my moves. Right as this is happening, I saw a few of my students nearby and heard one of them say, 'Kick his ass, Mr. Law.' It was quite a humorous moment in a very tense situation." Security quickly came to take control of the situation, and soon the police arrived to arrest the fellow. Later, Allan got word that the perpetrator was wanted on a murder warrant in Chicago.

During his teaching career, Law says he was out doing his volunteering from four p.m. to around midnight on most school nights and then would be out for about thirty hours on the weekend. Incredible. The number of volunteer hours is truly staggering. Just for the weekends, choose a low number of 10 hours per day, and that averages to 720 hours per year for thirty-six weekends. Figure that Allan spent ninety days each summer doing activities with the youth and, at a conservative average of 8 hours per day, that adds up to another 720 hours.

Let's say that we take a conservative number of hours (6 hours per afternoon/evening) volunteered from Sunday through Thursday night during his teaching career. That would be 30 hours per week. Multiply that by thirty-six school weeks and the hourly total is 1,080 per year or 34,560 hours during his career. Remember, these are low estimates.

When he speaks to groups, Allan is often asked where he goes to find the homeless. He never refers to specific locations or addresses. However, Allan estimates that he spends about 90 percent of his time in Minneapolis, 5 percent in St. Paul, and 5 percent in the first-ring suburbs. Up until COVID-19 hit, he usually drove a fairly familiar route, delivering sandwiches and clothing to his partner organizations, like Catholic Charities and the Salvation Army.

If he isn't headed for a specific drop-off location, Allan drives to places where he figures he'll find people who need help—under bridges, near freeway ramps, in or near abandoned buildings, near dumpsters, close to shelters, or in parks. He doesn't keep track but he estimates that he makes twenty-five to fifty stops a night.

Law figures he puts on an average of about fifty thousand miles a year on his current vehicle, a 2017 Ford van, but has put on as many as eighty thousand a year. It was donated by a man who wishes to remain anonymous, a fellow Allan met just once. This benefactor has donated two Chevy Suburban vans and also makes a sizable donation to the organization each year. At times, Allan alternates be-

Law driving on the streets of Minneapolis. (Courtesy of Jesse Roesler)

tween two different vans. He's easily driven more than a million miles over the past twenty-five years, most of it on the streets and byways of Minneapolis. He doesn't tire of the endless driving and yes, he does wear his seat belt.

Between all the work there is to do in trying to help the homeless, there are down times when Allan Law can catch a few winks. He estimates that he probably averages about two hours of sleep on his nightly forays on the streets. His most common time for sleep is around one a.m., and he might sneak in an hour. Law will park his van, put his seat back, and then call a friend at a gas station to tell that person to call him an hour later to wake him up. He will often repeat that scenario around five or six a.m., especially when he has had a sleepless day preparing for his night travels. He doesn't get that drowsy normally because he is in and out of his van so much; it keeps him alert.

Allan catching a few winks in his van. (Courtesy of Jesse Roesler)

Several years ago, he was stopped at a red light near Bobby and Steve's Auto World on 35W and Washington Avenue. The problem was that he was passed out. The cops knocked on his window and they recognized this familiar person. One of them said, "It's Mr. Law." An ambulance happened to be close by, and it was summoned to check on Allan. Sure enough, they checked his blood sugar and found out that he was diabetic. No more soda pop, I guess.

Those who are aware of Law's feeding and clothing efforts might not know that he also spends a considerable amount of time troubleshooting for those in need. Law takes calls from someone looking for help paying a utility bill, looking for temporary housing, or who is suicidal. Somebody needs help for their chemically dependent son, another needs a ride to see their dentist, and yet another can't afford a plumber to fix their leaking sink. Can you imagine taking as many as two hundred calls a day and having an expectation of then solving that problem or acting on it immediately? Before the onset of cell phones, of course, he had to rely on pay phones, and that was one-way communication. Many of the families and people he dealt with didn't even have a landline, so the ubiquity of cell phones has been a huge advancement.

"You can't believe all the people who need help out here," says Allan. "There are a lot of things happening in the middle of the night, but I'm on call twenty-four hours a day. I'm here to change lives, not just to feed more people."

Thus, the man with the horseshoe-shaped mustache, attired in his ubiquitous flannel shirt, keeps racking up the volunteer hours. It is almost unfathomable to consider. Back to the math. Since his retirement in 1999, Allan Law has spent twenty-five years on his beat. Figure 363 days per year times twenty-five years equals 9,075 days. Subtract 10 days per year for illness or injury, and that puts our total at 8,825 days. Let's assume 16 hours per day (many years were well above that), and that multiplies to 141,200 hours of volunteering. Averaging 18 hours per day, a more likely scenario, the total surges to 158,850 hours. Absolutely astounding!

In late 2017, WCCO TV aired a story about Allan Law and his organization. A viewer who wanted to remain anonymous donated a 2015 ten-passenger Ford van to the cause after learning that Allan's seventeen-year-old van had become unreliable. The Twin Cities family bestowed him this gift in memory of their son Nash. Doctors had diagnosed Nash with Duchenne muscular dystrophy at a

Allan Law with his donated van in Edina.

young age, and he died in April of that year at age seventeen. Nash found joy in every day and found happiness in helping others.

"It was a true blessing to receive a gift like this," remarks Allan when showing the author the vehicle. "I didn't even know this family, yet they wanted me to have it because this is what their son would want. I have a picture of him in the van. On the back of the van is #WWND: What Would Nash Do. A reminder to be kind and help others."

It is a beautiful van, and Law was overjoyed and humbled by the generosity. He started to utilize this fully equipped van but soon found that it was a little too difficult for him to get in and out of and maneuver the plastic bins. Unfortunately, it mostly sits idle in his condominium parking lot. Fortunately, he has had other benefactors provide for his driving needs and is currently alternating between two different vans.

Law with a friend on a cold winter night. (Courtesy of Jesse Roesler)

During the winter months, he purposefully checks out areas near bars and taverns after closing hours, anticipating there will be intoxicated people he may be able to help. "Sometimes, they may need a ride to the hospital or need some bus tokens to warm or take them to someplace safe," says Allan. "On other occasions, they may need a better winter coat, gloves, warmer socks, or knit caps. When the tent communities were prevalent a few years ago, I even bought a lot of wood to help them build fires. Of course, we give out a lot of blankets and boots during the severe cold."

In 2013, Allan was diagnosed with stage 4 prostate cancer. Successful surgery was performed at M Health Fairview Southdale Hospital in Edina, and he spent three days there before recovering at a nursing home in Bloomington for several days. It drove him crazy. Believe it or not, he snuck out of the rehabilitation center for a few nights of volunteer work, driving his own van while still in hospital garb. He also had his brother Lanny pick him up during that stay a couple times for the same purpose.

In 2016, the cancer reoccurred, and he had radiation at Fairview Southdale for thirty-eight days. In early 2019, it was detected yet again, and he started receiving experimental injections to continue to battle the disease. He was forced to slow down, which, of course, is relative in his case. His cancer is still present in his system, but he perseveres. By the summer of 2023, he looked better than he had for the past several years.

Despite all his health issues, Allan Law is determined to continue his mission. It is amazing that all his physical ailments haven't prevented him from his valiant efforts to alleviate hunger and poverty. "I know there are a lot of people who are praying for my health," remarks Law. "I have my health battles, but I have been blessed to have enough strength to forge forward, and I attribute that to God's grace. It is an answer to all the prayers said on my behalf. I will be out here until I'm no longer able."

Chapter Five

VOLUNTEER SPIRIT

Those who are aware of the story of Allan Law and his life of selfless service often wonder what sort of intrinsic motivation prompted him to such a life. Certainly, there must have been some religious fervor instilled in him as a child, or perhaps it was a life-altering event that spurred him to such dedication in early adulthood. Allan says, "My mother was a huge influence on me and always emphasized that the best thing I could ever do in life was to simply help people, in whatever way one could. Even as a youngster, I tried to help whenever there was a need.

"As for specifically helping the poor," Law continues, "I saw it on my first day of teaching in the fall of 1967. I was teaching fifth grade at the Field School (46th Street and 4th Avenue) in South Minneapolis. I did my student teaching in Edina, and the kids were all dressed nice and economically, were well-off. Right away, I witnessed the plight of so many of the kids I encountered in Minneapolis and felt I had to do something. Looking at the roster of my students, I saw a lack of fathers and learned they were living in some dumpy places and that there were some really tough situations.

"I told my principal that year that I would prefer to teach on the North Side of the city because there was even a greater need there," says Law. "I told him the South Side was too easy, and he told me that Field was one of the most difficult schools in the city. In my second and final year at Field, I had a student in my room named Frankie Richardson, and she is now sixty-six and serves on the board of my organization."

Pressed for his motivation for what he does, the ever-candid Law states, "It sounds crazy, but I just help people. It's that simple. I was helping people before I went to college. I always wanted to be a social worker but I found out, working with some of them, that they really weren't satisfied in what their life was, and they wanted to make a change. Many of them looked at themselves as highly paid clerical workers. They would tell me that 'we write checks but we don't see any results.' Many I worked with told me that I do more in a day than they did in two weeks because of some of the restrictions placed upon them."

Queried about where he gets the physical, emotional, and spiritual strength to maintain his incredible schedule, Allan adds, "I don't recall one day, over all these years, that I didn't want to go to work for these people. I suppose it's just something innate in me. I believe in God, and this is what he wants me to do: to help the poor, the unfortunate, and the needy. My mom and dad, of course, were big factors in my upbringing and outlook. Dad did a lot of work in our church and on different committees and in his role as a councilman and mayor in Richfield. Mom was very involved in the churches we attended, and her compassion for people ran deep.

"I accepted Jesus Christ as my Savior at a Billy Graham crusade at the State Fair as a fifteen-year-old," continues Allan. "We grew up going to Methodist church on Sundays in Minneapolis and then in Edina for a few years before moving to Richfield, where we joined the Wooddale congregation. My mom, especially, was a big supporter of my charitable activities. Dad, on the other hand, used to get on me about becoming the 'social worker of the city.' He used to ask what I was doing all this stuff for. For Christmas in 1969, when I was teaching on the North Side, I bought twenty-five hundred gifts and wrapped them and drove all around delivering them to the kids. Dad wondered why I was doing this when I was a teacher and said that I was crazy. I told him that teaching paid my bills, but helping others was my true job.

"No doubt," Law remarks, "I was different than all the other teachers, but the kids trusted me. The big advantage for me was that I was in the community and was involved and people knew where my heart was. The mothers got on my side, and they used to tell their kids to do what Mr. Law says."

Asked about the most important attributes for working with the poor, Allan replies, "I guess I can communicate with people who are homeless or destitute. Somehow, they have to know that you care, and I certainly do. I'm out there virtually every day and night with them, and it's the same way with kids; just be there for them and show an interest."

That said, how does a seventy-nine-year-old with cancer continually spend day and night helping the poor without totally breaking down? Law says, "I truly believe that God put me on this earth to help the poor. So, I get a cold or a headache, I still go to work. I don't care about my own ailments and problems." Not much can keep Law from his appointed task.

In November of 2023, however, Allan Law fell at about eleven thirty at night when completing his rounds. He was helped to his feet by two bystanders, but the injury was serious. He was driven to Fairview Southdale Hospital in Edina, and it was determined that he had fractured his left hip. After surgery, he was admitted to one rehabilitation center for two weeks before being placed in a rehab center in New Brighton near brother Lanny's house called Benedictine. He was confined there for nearly three months before he could manage to walk with the help of a walker.

"It felt like torture being in there because I could hardly move for the longest time, and the pain was excruciating. And, of course, I am not used to being 'cooped up' and not being out on the streets and dealing with people. Thank God that former student Trace Massie has done a fantastic job trying to fill the void, and I am so thankful for what he has done.

"I am having a real tough time physically, the worst pain since I got cancer in 2013. I've got painful knees, some missing teeth, and my whole body is a mess. But I've got to be out there every night, no exceptions. Until my hip fully recovers, I'll just put a wheelchair in my van so I can get around well enough to walk on my own. I might have to slow down a little, but I'm not giving it up."

The Sandwich Man handing out sandwiches on a brisk fall night. (Courtesy of Jesse Roesler)

Law overcame prostate cancer despite his exhausting schedule. He has also dealt with broken ribs from other falls in the past few years and currently has torn rotator cuffs in both shoulders. The Sandwich Man suffers from glaucoma and diabetes, and his nutrition is not ideal. As for that diet, Allan readily admits that there were far too many visits to McDonald's, especially with the kids. His typical meal might be a burger, fries, chips, and a soda. Toss in some high blood pressure and high cholesterol, and this guy has it all. Doctors have repeatedly told him that he needs to alter his eating habits and get more sleep—*much* more sleep. His body is suffering the trauma of an insane schedule.

Law's gait is slow, and he often appears ready to collapse. Despite his poor physical health, Law is undeterred. He states, "The doctors tell me I need certain surgeries, but

I don't have time for it. My body might be a wreck, but I am determined to continue to go out every night and serve people throughout the night and work during the day collecting food and clothing for them."

A proud yet humble man, Law is quick to deflect praise for his lifetime legacy of compassion and caring. He is aware that few people could do what he does, however. As for all the accolades, recognition, and praise he has received, he emphatically states, "I have never sought out any awards or applied to win some noteworthy honor; somebody else is doing that on my behalf. But it does help increase the awareness of the plight out there and helps out our donations, for sure."

Perhaps the first big recognition came in 1999 from KARE 11, which has sponsored the Eleven Who Care award for decades. Dennis Massie, Allan's former student, nominated him on behalf of the overall organization. Two weeks later, Law got a phone call indicating that he had been chosen as one of the award winners. The awards banquet was a formal affair at the Hilton Hotel in downtown Minneapolis, and older brother Larry remembers, "It was worth the price of a tuxedo to see Allan in one."

During the summer of 2000, Allan was notified that he would be traveling to Washington, DC, to be honored as one of the winners of the Jefferson Awards for Public Service. The awards were created in 1972 by the American Institute for Public Service. The nonprofit organization was established to honor individuals or organizations that have made significant contributions to public service or the community. The founders were Jacqueline Kennedy Onassis, Robert Taft Jr., and Samuel Beard. The Jefferson Awards are presented each year in a prominent location in the nation's capital, and a broad array of honorees are recognized.

No one from Minnesota had ever garnered that lofty prestige. Allan Law didn't want the attention and declined. He was eventually convinced to attend anyway. He had to buy a suit, as it was a requirement for the event. Plus, he had to learn how to tie a tie! Not so, as one of the employees at the fancy hotel they were staying at took care of that responsibility.

During the festivities at the US Senate chamber, Allan stayed in the background, scrupulously avoiding the limelight and those utilizing a camera. It wasn't important for him to "hang out" with the uppity. He aimlessly mingled among the East Coast elites. At the honorary banquet with big-name celebrities and dignitaries abounding, the forty-one honorees from all over the nation voted among themselves for one person to receive the Jacqueline Kennedy Onassis Award for Greatest Public Service Benefitting Local Communities. Allan was cited as the winner, quite an honor considering the awesome accomplishments of all the other nominees.

Law was literally stunned when it was announced that he was the winner of the so-called Gold Medallion Award, given to the person who best reflects the Jeffersonian ideals of citizen involvement and volunteerism that year. The following morning, he was presented the award at the Supreme Court chamber by Senator John Glenn of Ohio, the

Minnesotan Allan Law speaks at the US Supreme Court, 2000. (Courtesy of the Law family)

former astronaut. Law then proceeded to spend ten minutes speaking about his program and community service.

As a young man, Law was inspired by Martin Luther King Jr. and his message of peaceful nonviolence. Law says, "He didn't lead a perfect life, for sure, but there is no question what he did for civil rights for this country. I used to show the award-winning documentary on civil rights called *Eyes on the Prize* to my students, many of whom were Black, of course. I have no prejudice against any ethnic or national group, and I believe the Black community in the Twin Cities appreciates my efforts on their behalf. I deal with all kinds of minorities, including our own Native Americans, and it is sad to see the incredible level of poverty we see now. It is so much worse than thirty or forty years ago and getting worse all the time, especially the last few years with all the civil unrest, the COVID epidemic, the opioid crisis, mental illness issues, and the skyrocketing cost of housing."

Over the years, many people have called Allan "a living saint." He understands the thought and is humbled by it. "I have been called a saint by many people," he responds. "That includes a good friend of mine, Joe Selvaggio, who was a priest at Holy Rosary in South Minneapolis before leaving the priesthood. The first time I went to his home in South Minneapolis, he walked in a circle around the chair I was sitting in in his living room. I asked him what he was doing, and he tells me that despite traveling all over the world and being a priest for many years, it is the first time he was actually in the presence of a living saint.

"I told him he had to be kidding, and he told me he was dead serious," Law relates. "Whenever he would call me, he would ask if this was 'Saint Law' he was speaking to. I would say, 'No . . . no . . . no.' I have always enjoyed going to the Catholic schools and the Catholic churches because they don't have to follow all these ridiculous restrictions."

Can or has anyone else ever done what he has done? He immediately says, "No. The only person who approaches it is Mary Jo Copeland, and she has done it differently than me and she deserves a lot of credit. She does what I don't do, and she has inspired a lot of people to volunteer and to donate to help the less fortunate. She is a true hero, no doubt, and has been a real blessing to the Twin Cities scene. I don't mean to criticize her, but I wouldn't close at night and not be open on the weekend. We could have hundreds of people a night sleeping in sleeping bags."

*Mary Jo Copeland and Allan in the cafeteria at
Sharing and Caring Hands in Minneapolis.*

The author remarks, "I guess you two were sort of a dynamic duo—one by day and one by night."

Law laughs and says, "I guess that's a good way to put it." He then wants to make sure that he is not slighting Mary Jo and wouldn't want to disparage her work in any way. He adds, "It's just a lot different out there on the streets at night; I suppose we both have our own niche.

"Mary Jo is very dedicated and a great human being," continues Law about his compatriot. "It's really interesting how we have dealt with the issue of hunger and homelessness in similar yet very unique ways. The world has to appreciate all she has done for people in Minneapolis.

"I was over at Sharing and Caring Hands and Mary's Place a lot but never really talked at length with her," observes Law. "One time, we had the opportunity to talk for a while and we discussed what we were doing and how we did things. She told me that I was the craziest person she had ever heard about or known—in a good way, of course. She told me she wouldn't do what I did for a day. She told me that she didn't work at night, never on weekends, and certainly wouldn't go into areas I did. She remarked that I didn't have a building or staff to take care of, that I could just drive around and help people and that people were always talking to me."

And so it goes between the two Twin Cities titans in the world of helping the poor and the downtrodden. Each soldiers on, adding to their noteworthy status as legends in their own indefatigable manner. Great respect and admiration from one hero to another.

Living a life of service both night and day, Law is open about his feelings about the poverty that exists in today's society and his attempts to amend it. He is not afraid to make his observations known and is not fearful of admonishing both the public and private sectors for their failings in this regard. However, as he repeatedly contends, he is the only person out on the streets in the wee hours. He's not boasting; it's just a reality.

Since the onset of COVID, he has seen the closing of many facilities that house the poor and even the tent communities that abounded just a few years ago. Without becoming self-righteous, he is adamant that we have failed the downtrodden and the unfortunate. "Where else do we have NFL quarterbacks making forty-five million dollars a year and yet people are sleeping outside in the dead middle of the winter in frigid climates?" he inquires to the author.

Despite it all, however, he is still enamored of the "goodness" of humanity.

Doing what he has done has unequivocally meant true sacrifice. After all, from the start of his full-time work on the street upon his teaching retirement in 1999 until 2013 with the onset of a cancer diagnosis, Allan Law spent an average (yes, average) of eighteen hours a day procuring food or clothing for those in dire need. While his age and illness have limited him somewhat in recent years, he now laments that he is down to only working eighty-five to ninety hours some weeks. Those are just the nighttime and early morning hours. Seriously!

"My whole life has been a sacrifice to help the poor, but it has been my choice," says Allan without batting an eyelash. "I'm not able to see my brothers and their families as much as others or my friends, either. It's hard to have a relationship with anybody on a regular basis because of the schedule I keep. I really don't have friends because I don't have the time. I can't really get attached to anybody because there are so many people who need something from me."

I fall silent, for I feel sorry for this dedicated, compassionate man, and I am thankful for all the rich relationships I possess. Yet he is undeterred. I tell him that he has a million friends. He says succinctly, "My true friends are the people who have nothing." We both sit in the quiet for a while.

Then, the discussion shifts to female companionship, dating, and marriage. The author wonders how this could

Allan Law with one of his friends. (Courtesy of Jesse Roesler)

fit into his lifestyle, even when he was teaching and still spending another six to eight hours after school commiserating with youngsters and caring for the homeless while in his twenties and thirties. There had to be a woman or two, certainly, for this good-natured and exciting fellow. In our previous conversations, I never heard him mention much about his love life and his history with the opposite sex, with no mention of marriage for certain.

I am startled when he says, "I did get married, and it was the worst decision I ever made in my life. Nobody really knows about it. I was twenty-one years old and met this woman from St. Paul, and she falls totally in love with me. I had been a groomsman in my best friend Bob Noble's wedding, and other friends were getting married. So my gal Jo wanted to get married, and she convinced me to get married. I told her that I didn't know her that well, though we had been going out almost a year. It was a mistake because I really wasn't in love with her.

"I continued to teach and go out to do my work with the kids and the poor after we got married, and after several months it was over," Law says with little reticence. "I remember my grandmother telling me a few days before the wedding that I really didn't love this girl, and I concurred. I thought I shouldn't be getting married, but everybody else encouraged it. She was a nice girl. I would teach during the day and then go out entertaining with the kids at night. So we really didn't have much time together, and I was dead set on continuing to do what I was doing. We did see a marriage counselor, and I told her it wasn't going to work and we got divorced. We had the marriage annulled, and I haven't seen her since.

"I met other women after that, but there was one woman, Debbie, that I should have married," remarks Allan. "I met her at Bethel College, and my younger brother Lanny knew her. We would see each other, but then I would go out on the streets. In fact, she went on one of the trips out West one summer with fifteen Black kids in my six-passenger station wagon. I loved her, no question. But I wanted to continue my work at night. After we broke up, she married a year or so later and then was willing to leave her husband for me, but I couldn't do that—it wasn't or isn't right. Not marrying her bothered me for years, and then I stubbornly decided I wouldn't fall in love again." He had opportunities afterward to date women but stuck with the promise to himself not to get involved again.

Legacy is paramount to most people, and the Sandwich Man is no exception. Several years ago, there was a gathering at the Capri Theater, a reunion of former students, and Law was lauded by them. In a video posted at that event, nearly all the students cited him as their favorite teacher, and nobody had anything bad to say about him.

"I have a crazy sense of humor and like to confound people," admits Law, being interviewed at a bookstore near his condominium. "I like to make people think." Sure enough, he gets a call on his flip phone and, after the opening pleasantries, asks the person on the other end if they know where Delano and Willmar are located. He agrees to meet this person after our interview, and I ask him which city he is going to. Allan says, "Neither. I am meeting him in Minneapolis; I just asked him out of the blue if he knows where either city is." We both laugh.

A few seconds later, he asks if I have ever spent time in Stillwater. Is this trickster wondering if I have ever done time at the penitentiary? Yes, I state, at a few restaurants. He says he spent seven hours there. Where is anybody's guess.

What about this homelessness issue? Law says, "It is getting so much worse. We need more fathers in the homes. Mental illness is at least forty to fifty percent of the problem. Add to that alcohol and drug addiction, and that's another forty percent probably. And then you have people with financial issues. You can't judge who is homeless. There is little hope, especially for the way it is set up now. But this is my work. No vacations: too much work to do."

Law photographed at Barnes and Noble in Edina, March 2022.

To highlight the point about the homeless, Law relates a telling tale. Allan was on the street one night and came upon an elderly fellow. He proceeded to give the man a bus token, and the gentleman asked Law if he knew who he was. Allan said that he did not. The man told him that he was once a wealthy man and the CEO of a company. Then the casually dressed man told Allan that he had been a big donor to Love One Another. We sit in silence yet again as this information burrows into my brain . . . and heart.

Suddenly, Allan receives another call. It is a former student he had back in 1969–70 at Willard School. This gentleman, who just finished eight years in prison, is staying at a shelter and needs a place to live and a job. Allan Law has a fresh challenge. He tells me that he will be helping the former student as soon as we finish our conversation. Allan

Allan with his omnipresent flip phone at McDonald's, May 2023.

seems to always have some sort of plan for his days, but he must also be flexible, resourceful, and spontaneous to meet ever-changing demands for his services.

Meanwhile, back to the interview. When will he finish this work? A defiant answer: "Only when I die." Allan Law lives a simple life, and God provides what he needs. In an age of rising technology, where electronic devices are ubiquitous, this man runs a million-dollar organization that serves thousands a year with essentially no employees. He doesn't own a computer or a smartphone. As previously mentioned, Law is a difficult man to contact. He conducts his business on a forty-dollar flip phone from either Walmart or Target that costs thirty-five dollars a month for service. He gets four a year. Unfortunately, with all the calls he gets, his phone bank fills up, and callers cannot leave a message. It can be a problem getting access to him or attempting to communicate with him.

Despite the difficulty in setting up meetings or interviews, he is always engaging, funny, outspoken, and authentic. Most of all, he is a storyteller with a story. We'd need six volumes to contain all his tales. It is a pleasure to be in his presence, a real treat to sit one-on-one with a bona fide hero. On each occasion we meet, I am amused and entertained and totally astounded at his level of giving and sacrifice. He's a man to be admired, a man to be respected, a man to be emulated—wait, there is no one like him. No one.

Chapter Six

EARLY LIFE

A llan Eugene Law was the second oldest of five sons born to Loren L. and Arlene R. Law, who raised their family primarily in Richfield. Their first son, Larry Loren Law, was born on September 30, 1942, but died less than a month later on October 23. Allan's older brother, Loren Larry Law, was born on January 13, 1944, in Minneapolis. Allan became his Irish twin on New Year's Eve that same year, also at St. Mary's Hospital, when the temperature was 20 degrees below zero. Gregory Leo was born on August 20, 1946, and Lanny Lester Law on September 10, 1953.

Loren L. Law was born on February 8, 1917, in Bordulac, North Dakota. He graduated from Valley City State University in 1942 after studying business and instrumental music. Later in his life, he served as president of the alumni association. He taught high school for six years in North Dakota, starting two bands. He migrated to Minnesota and taught in Monticello for one year before moving to Minneapolis to work as a training director with Northwest Airlines in 1942. He was drafted into the Army in WWII, serving two years, mainly stateside, as an officer in the Air Corps. After receiving his Air Corps Officer Command in 1945 (training in New Mexico), Loren spent a year in New

Allan as a toddler. (Courtesy of the Law family)

York City in the Air Transport Command for the newly created Air Force.

After his military service, he returned to Northwest, where he stayed until 1953 before moving on to leadership roles at Archer-Daniels-Midland Company, Northwestern Refinery, and SuperAmerica as vice president of human resources from 1957 to 1970. In 1970, Allan's parents formed Loren L. Law & Associates, a management consulting firm specializing in executive searches and organizational studies for both the public and private sectors.

In 1969, the fifty-one-year-old Law was mowing his lawn in Richfield when residents showed up and asked him to run for the city council. He won. After three years of experience, he ran for mayor of the first-ring suburb and won again. He was mayor for eight years and oversaw a period of great growth—a new library, several new parks, and the development of permanent streets, among several prominent improvements. Loren Law Sr. served the city at a critical juncture, helping set the stage for major development. He also served as president of the Minnesota Mayors Association for two years.

In 1973, Law ran for office as a state representative on the Republican ticket but was unsuccessful. He lost in a bid for reelection as Richfield mayor in 1979 but spent all his time with the management consulting firm he founded with his wife, Arlene, a few years earlier. From Burnsville to Little Falls, Law used his experience as Richfield's mayor to help other cities, school districts, and companies recruit new leaders and run more efficiently.

Tom Hedges was working as St. Peter's city administrator in 1976 when Loren Law showed up at the twenty-seven-year-old's doorstep with a pitch: Would he be interested in leading a newly incorporated city called Eagan? "I didn't even know where Eagan was," says Hedges, who became Eagan's first city administrator, garnering a wonderful legacy of leadership himself and earning his city the reputation as an efficient and progressive enterprise before he retired in 2013. "Loren Law was able to discover people and help people as leaders in the public sector. He touched a lot of lives, and he certainly left his mark."

Arlene and Loren were active members at Wooddale Church, and he served as chairman of the deacons for many years. Allan's father loved cheering on the Gophers' athletic teams, especially the football team, and following the news in the *Foster County Independent*, his hometown newspaper in his native North Dakota.

Allan's mother, Arlene Rita McIlanie, was born on January 19, 1916, and died on March 7, 2010, at age 94. She and Loren were married for seventy-one years. "I could not have asked for a better mother," recalls Allan. "She was compassionate and cared about her kids. She cared more about other people than she cared for herself; she was all about what was best for Dad and for us boys, and then the neighborhood and her church. She was totally empathetic to others' concerns and was the most devout Christian I have ever known, and there is no question about that.

"My mother always said that the most important thing that you can accomplish in life is to care about other people," continues Allan. "Her goal was to get herself and her family to heaven, and she believed that one had to be a follower of Jesus Christ to do so and to follow what he said. She told her boys that she wanted to see us in heaven, so we had better do what we needed to in order to get there. Though she was definitely caring, she was firm in what she believed, and we boys knew the boundaries. I used to tease my dad and tell him that she would get into heaven just for putting up with him, and we would chuckle, and others told him the same thing."

To her sons, Arlene was a quiet, deeply spiritual woman who was especially warmhearted. She was apparently a wonderful friend to her husband, a loving mother, and a great listener and friend to others. Mrs. Law, along with Loren Sr., was also a very hard worker, and the couple were considered "servant leaders" in their church and community.

Youngest son Lanny remarks, "A favorite bible passage of Mother's was Proverbs 3:5–6—'Trust in the Lord with all your heart and lean not on your own understanding; in all your ways acknowledge Him and He will direct your paths.' This passage continues to be one of the most important guiding principles in my life, and I believe in the life of my brothers, as well."

Growing up, Loren and Arlene Law both attended small community churches in their respective small towns in North Dakota. In a small Methodist church in Valley City, North Dakota, the two made a serious decision to follow Jesus Christ as their Lord and Savior when Loren was attending college there. No doubt, their faith was their foundation, and their sons have continued that religious guide. Lanny concludes, "My parents' favorite verse is on my mother's gravestone and was on the memorial card at my father's funeral: 'Believe in the Lord Jesus, and you will be saved—you and your household.'"

Arlene Law's father was an alcoholic, and so was her maternal grandfather. Arlene made a pledge not to drink, and she never took a drop her entire life. When she was seventeen, her Irish-born father died from alcoholism and heart disease. Her mother, Nora, had to deal with severe medical complications, and Arlene was forced to grow up fast. Thus, Arlene grew up to be hardworking, responsible, and accountable.

Remarking on his parents' marriage and his childhood, Allan says, "We had a peaceful home upbringing; we were never really disciplined or spanked. It was just assumed

*Loren Law Sr. and his wife, Arlene, on their fiftieth
anniversary. (Courtesy of the Law family)*

that you were supposed to behave. My father liked to be
the boss and say we needed to do something a certain way.
Mother would usually give in, yet she would always have
something to say, and she was usually right. Dad liked to
think he set the rules, but he would acknowledge Mother's
wisdom too. They had a traditional marriage for that era,
but they were still a team."

"Mom and Dad didn't smoke or drink or even dance,"
Allan recalls. "When we were in grade school, none of the
boys had to square dance in elementary school because
Mother had us excused from that activity. She said that
dancing would lead to drinking and 'other things' that she
saw as a negative. Mom and Dad had seen it growing up
and were concerned about their own kids' futures."

Loren L. Law Sr. wanted his children to be exposed to
music, so he moonlighted selling Cutco cutlery and bought

a brand-new Lester piano, and all the boys took lessons. After forming that foundation, the Law youngsters started band lessons (Larry on the trombone and Allan, Greg, and Lanny on the trumpet).

"Like most people around us, we didn't grow up with a lot of money," Allan remembers. "I wanted a bike when I was seven years old and my father says then I better earn some money to buy one. I went door to door selling things, and I bought one. All of us but Lanny had paper routes. When I was ten or eleven, I went to North Dakota to live with my grandparents for the summer, and I would be driving the pickup hauling grain. Larry was up there, too, working in the field, and I drove the truck."

At age eighty-one, Loren L. Law retired, and he and Arlene spent the winters at a condominium on Singer Island near West Palm Beach, Florida. When he was eighty-seven, he wrote his autobiography, *The Life Story of Loren L. Law and His Faithful Wife Arlene*. He moved from Richfield in 1980 to live in an Edina condominium on York Avenue with Arlene, but they also split time during the warmer months at their cabin on Lake Sylvia in Annandale.

Loren L. Law died at age 101 on December 30, 2018, and was buried at Washburn-McReavy Hillside Cemetery in Minneapolis. According to son Lanny, their father could outwork all of his sons, even as an elderly gentleman. "The guy just never stopped," states Lanny. "He helped people lead and to get things done. He always said: 'Listen to the nobody just as much as the somebody,' and he embodied that all his life."

To Lanny, who gave a rousing eulogy at his father's funeral, three things were evident throughout his long life. "First," says Lanny, "was that Dad was a man of action, and he wanted to do things right. All through his long life, he was a leader and someone that simply got things accomplished. Raised in a small town in North Dakota, he was a leader in the community as a boy, delivering newspapers, milking the family cows, being a leader at school as a basketball player or having the lead role in the school play.

"Second, Dad was a man of integrity," adds Lanny. "He did not cut corners, and he led by example, whether as a father, coach, or citizen. He coached all of his boys in basketball and baseball. And because he and my mother both had fathers who abused alcohol, neither he nor my mother ever used alcohol—either in the house or at social gatherings. As Dad's friends and coworkers knew, they would always have a sober designated driver in my mother and father.

"Third, Dad never forgot about growing up in a small town and being a down-to-earth person," states Lanny. "At my father's funeral, I brought up the latest issue of the *Foster County Independent*, the county paper for all the small communities, including Bordulac, where Dad was raised. He continued to subscribe to that newspaper to keep up with all the things happening there."

Allan remarks, "My dad was a hard worker, and he was always helping people; if there was a problem, he was going to take care of the problem. Both Mom and Dad would walk in their neighborhood and pick up garbage. Dad was always on time and the most organized person I have ever known. I have records that he kept from as far back as his college days, impeccably filed. And as his son, I might be the most disorganized person ever, truly.

"My dad, however, never completely understood my commitment to helping the poor," adds Allan. "I remember one time I brought twenty-five kids from the inner city out to the family cabin, and he didn't understand why I just wouldn't come by myself to relax. I told him that I have to help people, and he couldn't grasp why in the world I would do what I was doing. Mother understood and was so accommodating to the boys and girls I brought out there, and they had a whale of a time. However, after Mother passed, I would come into his condo at about noon after a long night on the streets, and he would say, 'Well, tell me about your night.' So he was starting to accept and appreciate what I was doing. For the last several years of his life, he was so gracious in thanking me for checking on him every day and said that he wouldn't be alive or might be in a nursing home without my concern."

The Law family lived in South Minneapolis when they moved from Monticello when Loren Sr. was employed at Northwest Airlines. Their first domain was at 4808 14th Avenue South, near Minnehaha Parkway and Minnehaha Creek, and the boys attended nearby Northrop School. When the younger Loren was in sixth grade, the Laws moved to eastern Edina. The three-bedroom home was located at 5832 Chowen, ten blocks north of Southdale Shopping Center.

Loren Jr., commonly referred to as Larry, remembers,

"They were just starting to build Southdale at that time. Our family was a traditional middle-class family at the time: Mom the typical housewife at home, and Dad worked hard to provide for us. Dad taught us about having a strong work ethic, and he loved sports, so we always found a sports event to attend, listen to, or watch. We lived in Edina for about four years, and all four boys attended Edina public schools."

The oldest three boys were active in Little League baseball. Larry played third base, Allan pitched and played the outfield, and Greg was a left-handed pitcher. They were fortunate to have a large backyard with no alley, so they had a lot of room for playing ball. The Law boys also played on their successful church basketball team, which once lost the city championship by just two points. In 1957, Loren Sr. and Arlene purchased a lake lot on Lake Sylvia near Annandale, Minnesota. They didn't build a cabin on it for three years, but the property eventually became a wonderful place for them to frequent during the warmer months.

"Both my parents were very religious and strong in their faith," says Larry. "It seemed like everybody back then was a traditional churchgoing family, and we attended Asbury Methodist Church. It was very close to Forty-Fifth Street and Bloomington Ave South, and the Laws were very involved there, and the oldest three boys were all confirmed there. Later, we started going to Wooddale, which was located in Richfield. Mom was committed to teaching Sunday school always; in fact, she was named the Sunday School Teacher of the Year in 1967 at a national convention

*Greg (left), Lanny (baby), Larry, and Allan, circa
1954. (Courtesy of the Law family)*

right here in Minneapolis. She was also a community Bible
study leader for women from all over the Twin Cities in an
organization called Bible Study Fellowship.

"When I was in ninth grade, we moved to Richfield
and lived at 6414 11th Avenue, a brand-new five-bedroom
house," recalls Larry. "We all attended Minnehaha Academy on East River Road in South Minneapolis. I made a
deal with my parents that I would pay half of my tuition if
they paid for the other half.

"Baseball was the only organized sport that Allan
played," says Larry. "He did play a lot of church basketball,
but he never went any further and didn't play any sports in
high school. When he and I were in fifth and sixth grade, we
started to make a few bucks shoveling snow, cutting lawns,
and delivering newspapers. As you know, brothers can get
into some pretty good battles, but I think we got along bet-

ter than most brothers. There were never any memorable battles, and we all still get along really well today."

Larry, now eighty, adds, "Allan was always a fun guy with a good sense of humor, and he was not only very bright but a real character too. Even when he was young, he always wanted to do things to the fullest. In high school at Minnehaha Academy, he played trumpet in the band and had to complete his share of fundraising. He had to sell ten dollars' worth of candy, and he went all over the neighborhood and to office buildings and ended up selling more than five hundred boxes of chocolate bars.

"One night when he was in high school, the Richfield police brought Allan home after a tomato-throwing incident," Larry recalls. "Nobody would have pegged Allan to be voted Most Likely to Succeed at Minnehaha despite his intelligence; he just didn't apply himself. But just look what he has accomplished."

Allan recalls, "I never had any real close friends except for Bob Noble, mostly because I was either working or going out on a date. People knew me as kind of a jokester, and I would do things to make them laugh or confuse them. I was probably known as the so-called 'class clown,' but I didn't feel good about myself because I had some physical problems that caused me to be out of sports. It was called 'pigeon chest' and even kept me out of the Army because I flunked my physical. So I wasn't involved in athletics in high school, and though not a great athlete, I would have been competitive.

"I was a pitcher in baseball, a right-hander," adds Allan.

"I remember Wayne Courtney, the well-known Roosevelt basketball coach who had won two state titles for them. He was in charge of the Edina baseball program—knew Dad well—and he later became the mayor of Edina, and they had a lot of contact with each other.

"I played the trumpet in the band at Minnehaha Academy," Allan states. "Because I had braces, I played the baritone, and we got to go to the World's Fair in Seattle at the end of my senior year in 1962. I marched in the parades, and that was a really big deal. I used to say that I was never any good; I just carried the baritone. I did sell the most candy for our band trip and should have gone into sales because I was a born salesman with my personality; I sure would have made a lot of money."

"Once Allan started teaching, he wanted to go to the toughest school with the most challenging students," adds Larry. "Sure enough, after a few years at Field, he requests to go to a school with a higher racial mix. Regarding race, he doesn't look at people as Black, white, or anything else; he just sees them as people. Throughout his career, he wanted to deal with the 'have-not' students, no matter their ethnic or racial background. He taught kids to be appreciative and thankful, and to this day, his former students all refer to him as . . . Mr. Law.

"Our family is very proud of what he has done, of course, but he just sort of brushes it off," says his older brother. "He just thinks that this is what he was put on the earth to do, to help people. I couldn't do what he does and don't know anybody who could except him. Can you imagine the energy it takes to do what he does every single day and night? I don't think he's ever done anything solely for himself. He thinks about the plight of others and how we can meet their basic needs, and then he goes out to personally deal with it.

"Allan is the most caring individual I have ever met," states a sincere Larry. "He saw a need in the community, and he singlehandedly went about trying to solve it. It takes a tremendous amount of drive and belief to do what he does every day, and he just perseveres. He's out on the street all night, but then he is doing things during the day, too, like speaking to school groups and companies and picking up supplies. It is an amazing story."

Allan on Larry: "He has been very successful in his financial career, yet we don't have a lot in common. But I know if I needed help, he would be there for me. I don't see him for months at a time, but I talk to him quite a bit. He calls to ask me what I need, and he is very generous in supporting my programs."

Larry Law was a fine student and a star athlete in football, basketball, and track for the Redhawks, graduating in 1961. He worked at SuperAmerica during the summers in high school and during his college years at the University of Minnesota. After graduating from the U of M in 1965, he was employed at Mobil before joining Blair & Associates, an investment firm. After moving to the Hornblower company, Larry hitched on with Dain Bosworth, now known as RBC Wealth Management, for a ten-year tenure.

Today, Larry lives in Plymouth with his wife, Carol, and continues his sixteen-year tenure as a senior vice president with Robert W. Baird Company, a private wealth management firm. He spent twenty years in the same capacity for Piper Jaffray. Larry Law, who now spends most of the winter at his condominium in Singer Island, Florida, has two children, Danny and Debbie, and each have three children of their own.

Lanny Lester Law, now seventy-one, lives in New Brighton with his wife, Maureen. They both serve as psychotherapists, even collaborating on a book in 2002 about marriage called *God Knows Marriage Isn't Always Easy*. Lanny is employed by Nystrom & Associates in New Brighton and is a licensed marriage and family therapist, still working at least three days a week. For the past few years, he has served as the administrative assistant for Love One Another and as a volunteer, picking up and delivering sandwiches and other donations.

As a young child, the youngest Law boy had developed a deformed hip from Perthes disease, which prompted him to have to wear a leg brace for more than two years. Because the Chowen residence was on a large hill, the family began investigating relocation to a house that was on flat ground. Thus, when Lanny was three years old, the Laws moved into a newly built home at 6414 11th Avenue South in Richfield. It was, indeed, on flat land adjacent to Legion Lake, a swampy area between 11th Avenue and Portland Avenue.

Behind the Law home was a large field between their property and Legion Lake. The neighborhood developed it into a place called "Lannypolitan," a reference to the youngster's love of baseball and nearby Metropolitan Stadium in Bloomington, where the Twins then competed. Kids from all over 11th Avenue and its environs gathered to play their own baseball games. They would often have teams from nearby neighborhoods come and join them for competitive games.

After becoming the fourth Law son to graduate from Minnehaha Academy in 1972, Lanny enrolled at Bethel and earned a BS degree in psychology in 1976. Despite his leg problems as a youth, Law went on to play four years in high school in football, basketball, and tennis. At Bethel, he lettered four years in tennis and one in football. He then spent six weeks the summer after his college graduation on a mini-missionary project in Dublin, Ireland. There he met a young woman from Ireland named Maureen Rogers, who would become his future wife.

Upon his return to the United States, Lanny worked for six months in a halfway house as a certified chemical dependency counselor in St. Paul, helping people recover from alcohol and drug addiction. That work prompted him to enter Bethel Seminary, receiving his master of arts degree in theological studies in 1979. Faculty members encouraged him to further enrich his spiritual education, so he pursued his master of divinity degree from McCormick Theological Seminary in Chicago (1980), a Presbyterian school on the University of Chicago campus. Lanny received a free fellowship to Colgate Rochester Crozer Divinity School in Rochester, New York, and he received his doctor of ministry degree in the spring of 1982.

Rev. Law served as pastor at Lakeside Baptist in Duluth, Minnesota (1983–89) and then as senior pastor at Oak Hill Baptist in Columbia Heights (1990–2000). In 1999, Lanny Law left pastoral ministry to take a full-time position at Nystrom, a large Christian counseling center, where Maureen was employed for twenty-four years before her retirement. During his two pastoral jobs, Lanny also worked part-time at Lutheran Social Services.

Lanny, like his brothers, had a profound respect for his father and mother. "Having been deeply loved by both parents, who also set an example of servanthood to their children, it positively affected me and my brothers," states Lanny just a scant few weeks after his father's funeral. "They were committed to God, committed to be good people, and to also serve others."

Certainly, the Law boys were influenced greatly by their parents. Their outlook and philosophy were ingrained in them at an early age, especially to have a strong work ethic, to be good Christians, and to care about others. As Loren Sr. wrote in the foreword to his book, "Arlene and I accepted the Lord in a small church in Valley City, North Dakota, in 1942 and the challenge now falls to our children, grandchildren, and great-grandchildren, and those who follow them . . . to honor God and to be honest in all their dealings that there may be no broken link in the family chain—'Believe in the Lord Jesus Christ and thou shalt be saved, and thy house'—Acts 16:31."

Certainly, Allan Law was listening to and observing his parents in action as a youngster and young man. He was a

The Law boys with Lanny in his toy car, circa 1956.

mentor to Lanny, and the younger brother is appreciative. Says Lanny, "Allan has always been my dearly beloved brother from my early childhood right through the present. When I developed the hip disease, my mother and father and brothers had to make sure I would never be on my feet without the brace on. My father often traveled with his job and had many long work hours, so taking care of a young, physically disabled child was a major job for my mother.

"Allan was my mother's assistant," continues Lanny. "He has always had such a caring heart for people, and he really showed this to me while growing up and even in my adult years, as well as being a second father to my own four children. When I was small, we both watched the local professional wrestling shows, and then we would start wrestling ourselves. I would pretend to be Verne Gagne and Allan would put a pillow in his shirt and pretend to be Haystack Calhoun, an extremely large man. While I still had my brace on, Allan bought me a small toy car that I could ride in; he had spent all the money he had saved from delivering newspapers.

"Allan has always been a caring person throughout his life and in all areas," adds Lanny, who finds his older brother to be giving, spontaneous, flexible, adaptable, and compassionate. "He does not compartmentalize his life whereby he is outwardly caring in some social situations and then acts differently behind the scenes in others. He is devoted to caring for others. When the feature-length film *The Starfish Throwers* was developed several years ago, it highlighted Allan along with two other inspiring individuals. Promotional magnets were made, and the statement on his read: 'The most important thing in my life has always been to bring happiness to others.' This is a true statement of my brother Allan and who he is."

As the chairman of the board of Love One Another, Lanny Law is often asked about the future of the organization when Allan cannot continue in his present role. The younger Law says, "Love One Another so much reflects the life of Allan Law that it would have to change. Who else could possibly do what he does? Like any other organization that loses its founder, what the new chapter will look like, nobody knows. It's not important that the activities of the organization will be done in the same way; what is important is that the mission of Love One Another continues.

"The organization will never go wrong if we simply follow our mission," says Lanny Law. "If the activities look different and are done in different ways by different people, so be it. We just have to live out the vision. Our family is so proud of Allan and all of his accomplishments. Of course, for all he has done to help the less fortunate but also for being such a great family man as a son, brother, and uncle."

Allan, too, has a deep fondness for Lanny to this day. "I was real close with him when he was little and dealing with his illness. I had to help Mom out because he couldn't put any weight on the one leg. He would wear the brace, but he couldn't have it on all day. He has done real well in his life in all respects and I am certainly proud of him and his family."

Allan Law has two nephews and five nieces and is close to them despite his lack of time because of his commitment to his organization. Of Lanny and Maureen's children, both Christine and Erin have two children, while Kathleen gave birth to a new daughter in 2023 and son Kevin is single.

"I attended a lot of their events and activities, especially when they were younger," states Allan. "I used to babysit for them a lot, and we had a good time. Sometimes, I would let them stay up real late, but as soon as I heard the garage door go up, I would scurry them off to bed before their parents got inside the house. They are all good kids and were raised well."

Allan's brother Greg, a year and a half younger, was a highly successful financial advisor in the Twin Cities before moving permanently to Riviera Beach, Florida, about twenty-five years ago. Greg, also a Minnehaha graduate, matriculated to Mankato State, where he earned a BS in business management. After a stint at Prudential Insur-

*Loren Sr. and Arlene in 1997; Larry, Lanny, Allan, and
Greg (left to right). (Courtesy of the Law family)*

ance Company, Greg became a leading salesman at Dain
Bosworth and retired as a vice president. Allan remarks,
"Greg and I got along pretty well as kids and as adults, too,
but I haven't seen him much since he moved. However,
he does have a condo in the same building as me, and he
comes up for a few months in the summer." Greg and his
wife, Paulette, have a daughter named Heidi.

Queried about whether he regrets not being married and
becoming a father, Allan states, "I always truly loved kids
and think I would have been an unbelievable father, but I
realized, how could I be a father with eight kids at home
and still be out on the streets at night? I couldn't do both, so
I knew what I had to do. It was a very conscious decision to
give up becoming a husband and father. I don't regret my
decision, but it has been a real sacrifice."

Chapter Seven

SCHOOL DAYS

Allan Law went to elementary school at Northrop in South Minneapolis, from kindergarten through fourth grade, when his family lived on 14th Avenue South. He attended Wooddale in Edina for grades five and six and then spent grades seven and eight at Edina Junior High School. Law recalls, "I was just a normal kid growing up like everybody else. Wherever we lived, there were a lot of neighborhood kids, and we played in large groups in our yards. We played a lot of baseball and some basketball too."

Allan started attending Minnehaha Academy as a sophomore in 1959–60 after attending Richfield Junior High School for ninth grade. Older brother Larry was already establishing himself as a fine student and athlete at the noteworthy private school on River Parkway in Minneapolis. It seemed logical for Larry's Irish twin to attend also.

Of course, he couldn't be involved in athletics, and that affected his standing in his own eyes. He says, "Larry and his group were all athletes and hung out together, but I didn't have that and wondered where my place was. I dated a girl named Nancy that was in his group, however.

"I do remember one kid who had cerebral palsy," spoke Allan. "His name was Larry Lexville, and he couldn't walk,

Allan in his Little League uniform. (Courtesy of the Law family)

of course. He ate lunch by himself because no one else would, so I started to hang around with Larry. Nancy asked me why I would do that and I said, because it was important. We became good friends, but when I graduated, I lost contact with him. I later found out that he committed suicide.

"I went to school and passed my classes, but my grades were terrible," a smirking Law added. "I didn't hand in assignments and didn't do enough to excel in the classroom. I just didn't feel good about myself. I didn't feel any confidence in my intelligence, just felt very inferior in the academic area. Certainly, I was probably comparing myself to Larry, but I never let people know what I was thinking.

So I became a jokester and an entertainer, because it felt good to make people laugh and to make them feel comfortable." Always up for a good time, Allan also fondly recalls hosting a New Year's Eve party at his house for a couple of years while at Minnehaha that over thirty kids from the school and his neighborhood attended.

Despite the feeling of not belonging and being in another stratosphere, Allan Law used his moxie and his caring nature to start building a different legacy for himself. He started to realize that he had a natural affinity for helping others. Despite his avowed lack of academic or athletic identity, he was stacking good works up in his social tower. He comments, "I was always on the lookout for a chance to help and, of course, there are all sorts of situations to help people. I guess I found that this was my niche in life. Others around me knew that I cared about people."

Thus, late in his high school years, he began to think about becoming a social worker or a teacher. "I just wanted to change lives," says Law. "It really isn't that complicated; just start by being welcoming and friendly to everyone and respecting them as a person. Then, just be kind and considerate and show some interest in them. It would be a much better world if everybody could do that. Think of others and help in whatever way you can. It's as simple as that."

As mentioned previously, his best friend in high school was Bob Noble, a man he has great respect for. Allan remembers, "We were both in the band and were in a few classes together. We both liked the gals, of course, and we used to double-date. Bob was a good guy but very gullible, and I gave him a hard time, all the time. One time on a double date, we are walking up the sidewalk to his date's house and he says, 'Al, what is this girl's name? I forgot it,' and I say, 'It's Gloria.' Of course, her real name was not Gloria. Another time, I gave him instructions for where to go to pick up another girl and it led to him falling in the rosebushes; it was hilarious!"

Noble, who still lives in Minneapolis, grew up in the southeast part of the city and attended Sidney Pratt Elementary and Ramsey Junior High School before enrolling at Minnehaha Academy. Bob had a twin brother named Richard, but he associated with a different crowd.

Bob recalls, "I met Allan in tenth grade, and he became my best friend; he was definitely outgoing, and his priority was being a social animal. I was shy and pretty reserved and he was the opposite, so I liked that, and I would laugh at the things he would do. It was all innocent stuff, though. People were amused by him, and he was in the 'cool' group.

"In class, Allan was known by the teachers to definitely be a jokester," continues Noble. "One time, he pretended that he couldn't take it anymore, and he proceeded to jump out of an open window. He did, but there was a ledge underneath the window that he knew about, of course, but it certainly gave the teacher and the students a scare. He loved to do things like that. Occasionally, we would get out of English class to head to the counselor's office, telling the teacher that we were interested in getting into Harvard or Yale, but we were just trying to ditch class."

Noble, who also wrestled at Minnehaha, says, "I don't

think Allan could be embarrassed back then, and he still doesn't care what people think about him. We double-dated in high school and college, and it was sure fun. He set me up with several girls from First Covenant Church, but we also went to other churches and dated girls there too. We went to Christian youth meetings on Sunday nights and to sing-alongs in the summer.

"When I was a junior, I was riding with guys named Bill Erickson and Bill Sherwood," recalled Law. "Erickson was driving an old Chevy that evening and he said, 'Let's pick up some tomatoes and throw them at cars.' I said, 'I'm not going to do that; it's stupid.' I didn't know that they had already picked up some and started throwing them at cars from the front. I was in the back seat, and there wasn't a window I could even roll down. The park police picked us up and brought us to the police station. So I get in trouble, and I didn't throw anything, though I have to say I probably would have if I had any tomatoes in my possession. I don't remember that there was any action taken against us."

More than sixty years after her high school graduation from Minnehaha Academy, Apple Valley resident Mary Ann Brooks (formerly Rosdahl) still has fond memories of Allan. "We met as sophomores and I had him in one or two classes each of those three years and saw him around school," remarks Brooks. "As a young man, he was definitely fun and lighthearted and constantly cracking silly, corny jokes. He was quite the character, for sure, but he was never unkind and never made fun of people. No doubt, he was very well-liked."

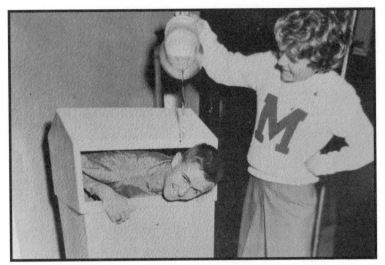

*Law was named Most Mischievous during his senior
year at Minnehaha Academy, along with Pam LaVine.
(Courtesy of* The Antler, *Minnehaha Academy, 1962)*

Perusing through Minnehaha's yearbooks (*The Antler*) from yesteryear, Brooks adds, "Allan was voted Most Mischievous our senior year, and it was certainly earned; he was always in motion and always up to something. Allan was consistently the last person to get to class, and I recall that he never had a pen or pencil and didn't take his classes that seriously. He was sort of wild, but he was very outgoing and friendly to everybody. He may have even asked me out, but I can't recall."

A long-time airline employee, Mary Ann states, "Allan was in the band and was in his wheelhouse at all the athletic contests with his fun personality and outgoing demeanor. He just loved people and wanted to make them feel good. He has always been sincerely interested in others, so I am not surprised by all that he has done. I guess you could call him

Senior photo, Allan Law, Minnehaha Academy,
1962. (Courtesy of the Law family)

a perpetual Good Samaritan. His commitment is so admirable, and to still be doing what he does at his age and with all the health concerns he has endured is really unbelievable."

Allan either got a ride with his brother's group or hitchhiked to school and then would usually hitchhike home, a common occurrence in the early 1960s. It was right up Law's alley, so to speak. A kid needed a ride home from school? Give him a ride as far as you could go. People helping people, with almost no fear of what might take place. A different time, no doubt.

Following graduation from high school, Allan enrolled

at the University of Minnesota in Minneapolis. Although social work and teaching were still paramount in his mind, he wasn't 100 percent sure, so he decided to enroll in General College, which allowed students to take coursework without designating a major.

"I wasn't exactly sure what I wanted to do, so it was nice to have the time to decide," says Allan. "I lived at home and commuted in an old red Volkswagen; it was my first car. I drove with the window down because there was no heater. I would almost be at school before the defroster started working. I really didn't get to know many people because I was working all the time."

During the summers through high school and college, Allan worked at Northwestern Refinery in St. Paul Park, where his father was employed as the vice president. "I did all of the physical work as a laborer," remarks Allan. "It was fun to do a lot of different things, but I made sure I worked hard out of respect for my dad. He made sure I took the job seriously, as he was the one who got me the job. At both the refinery and at the station, I was given the most difficult tasks, and I did them well."

Buddy Bob Noble also attended the U in the fall of 1962 and played tuba in the marching band for two years before transferring to Northwestern Bible College and then Bethel, earning his elementary education degree. Meanwhile, Allan was a groomsman when Bob married Marcia in 1966.

Marcia recalls how she and Bob got back at Allan for all of his dating pranks the year before their marriage. She giggles about the memory of it fifty-eight years later. "I had a coworker I was going to set Al up with, and she was a lot of fun and very spunky," she recalls. "I asked her to dress up real dowdy-like and look as bad as she possibly could when Allan showed up. I think she even wore a wig. So Allan meets her at the door and gets a look at this frumpy-looking girl, and he gives Bob a few cursory looks, like 'How could you do this to me?' My friend then excuses herself to change into a nice outfit and put some makeup on, and she looked absolutely dazzling. She comes back out to the door and says, 'Sorry to keep you waiting, Allan,' and we all had quite a laugh."

Meanwhile, Allan was getting a bit restless again, still living at home and attending school at the U. He was already involved in some social work in the evenings, but after two years, Law transferred to St. Cloud State. It wasn't a good fit, and he left after a quarter and transferred again to UW-River Falls. He earned his BS in elementary education and also minored in sociology, graduating in the spring of 1967.

A real influential person at River Falls was a Black gentleman who impressed the young Minnesotan. "Professor Bailey was very cool; he walked in with no socks on with his loafers and he never had any notes," recalls Law. "He didn't need any because he was that well-read. Even then, he was surprised how much I knew about Black history. Back in high school, I had thoughts about going down South to help with the civil rights movement and voting rights. I could have been one of those freedom riders, but I was working all the time."

Chapter Eight

TEACHING CAREER

"I student-taught fifth grade in Edina, and I loved the kids and they loved me," states Law. "They were great kids from good families, but I knew I couldn't teach there. It was too easy and too comfortable. I needed to teach in the inner city to make a real difference."

Allan Law began his teaching career as a substitute teacher at the Field School in South Minneapolis in the fall of the 1967–68 school year. A familiar figure joined him in 1968–69; it was Bob Noble, who student-taught there because Allan was already working there. Field School, located at 46th Street and 4th Avenue, was the first school in the city to be integrated with forced busing. Bob started teaching fourth grade there and ended up teaching fourth through sixth grade at Field for thirty years. Bob also taught twelve years of fourth grade at Minnehaha Academy following his public school tenure.

"I taught with Allan for two years at Field," says Noble. "No doubt, all the kids wanted to be in his class and he was fun. Then, Allan left for another school and our teaching careers never intertwined after that." Law requested a transfer to Willard Elementary in North Minneapolis in order to have more of an opportunity to work with minority children in the sixth grade. More teachers were trying to get

116

Law, first-year teacher in 1967–68. (Courtesy of the Law family)

out of the so-called "poorer" schools than in them, so the request was granted.

Noble says, "In the summer of 1969, I was working in a machine shop in the city and Allan was working for the Minneapolis Park Board as a part-time officer. He told me there were openings, so I applied and got the job. Allan was only with them for a couple years."

That break had Noble working at Minnehaha Falls as an officer the rest of that summer and started him on a thirty-two-year career with the Park Board. Bob served as an officer for several years but then became a Minneapolis Park Patrol agent and then the supervisor of the agents for many years. Noble enjoyed his years with the Park Board as he enjoyed the kids and lived close to the work. Meanwhile, he and Marcia started to have a family (eventually there were four children), and he even worked a third job for five years as a security guard at Methodist Hospital.

"Once we had children, we had no time and Allan was exceptionally busy, too, with all his activities," says Noble. "He was out doing his thing so I didn't see him much for quite a while. When I was finishing my teaching career at Minnehaha, I saw him more often and then at the gas station on occasion. We have wonderful memories, but our lives haven't really melded together."

Pondering all that Allan Law has accomplished, Bob Noble is not surprised. He states, "I'm not really surprised because he has been so committed to his cause. It is real to him and has become a part of who he is. Once he had two or three years doing his work, I knew he would be in for the long haul. His longevity is so amazing, considering all the health issues he has endured. Factor in the dangerous areas he cavorts in, and he has remained very safe. That indicates the trust and faith that the community has in him.

"There is no question that Allan Law is a free spirit, but you have to be unconventional to do what he has done and is still doing," continues Noble. "His priorities have always been to work with kids and now the homeless and that everything will fall into place because of his trust in the Lord.

He's out there, and he certainly has his opinions, but he can back it up with facts and all his experiences."

As for his legacy, Noble adds, "Boy, he is so loved by so many in Minneapolis, especially the Black community, for all that he has done for them. He always told me that he could go into any area because they knew him and trusted him, so he felt safe. He has left his whole personal life behind so he can pursue his real love—to be there for the people in need. Think about all the limitless hours he has poured into his organization, it's just amazing. I totally respect Al for what he has done: for his commitment, sacrifice, and focus in helping people. I think he would rather die out there doing his work than retiring and leading a life of leisure."

Mr. Allan Law spent many hours in the late afternoons and early evenings after school with his students and their families, in addition to weekends and the summer months, of course. Bolstered by his teaching salary, Law spent much of his own money providing for the needs of those youngsters and their neighborhood friends. In addition to food, he started to disperse clothing, footwear, school supplies, personal hygiene items, and whatever he felt was necessary.

In his first or second year teaching in Minneapolis, Allan Law was called to the district office for a meeting with the assistant superintendent. Allan recalls, "The fellow complimented me on all the good work I was doing with the students. I thanked him, and then it got quiet and a little uncomfortable. He told me that there had been some concerns

*Minneapolis Recreation Development crew on a boat
cruise on Lake Sylvia at the Law family cabin in
Annandale, 1980s. (Courtesy of the Law family)*

about me in my time outside school, that I was spending too much time with the 'colored' kids. I clearly told him that it was my business and that I would be continuing to do so. Never heard another thing about that issue.

"When I was teaching in North Minneapolis, I lived one house north of Bryant and Broadway," continues Law. "I was living in a rooming house because it was cheaper. The lady who operated the place kicked me out because she said there were too many 'colored' kids coming up to my apartment. Somehow, the kids found out I was living there, even though I never told them."

After a year at Willard, he transferred to Anwatin School in North Minneapolis for twelve years (1969–81), which switched from a middle school to a junior high school during his time there, but he continued to teach sixth grade.

He then transferred to Hall School on the North Side, but when that building closed, he finished his career working for thirteen years at Andersen United Middle School, near Abbott Northwestern Hospital.

Allan recalled, "Mr. McCoy, one of my assistant principals, called me the 'Miracle Man.' I asked him why, and he told me that whenever there was a problem with a student or parent or some administrative issue, they called on me to help. I kept them in line and motivated the students to do their best. I never pitied the kids from poverty-stricken families or those in need because everybody needs accountability and discipline."

In the classroom, Dennis Massie was thoroughly enthralled with this fellow. "He was certainly a fun teacher and always a jokester," remarks Massie. "He would teach by using real-life examples because he lived in reality, and he was constantly planting seeds of ideas in us. However, he was all about respect; his general rule was that he would respect us and that we, in turn, would respect him and others. We were to be accountable and to pass it forward. He was a godsend to me and all his other students, and we were blessed to have him as a teacher and model."

Dennis Massie's brother Trace concurs. "I was in Mr. Law's fifth-grade class at Sheridan, like Dennis the year before me, and there were only a few Black children in the school at the time. The kids, all the kids, couldn't get enough of him. As much as we liked our regular teacher, we wanted Mr. Law to stay."

Frankie Richardson, who has served on the Love One

Another board for the past ten years, met Law for the first time as a ten-year-old at the Field School in 1968. She was a fourth-grader in a class across the hall from Law's fifth-grade classroom and witnessed Law in action that first year. The following year, she was one of Law's students. A Black woman, she has vivid memories of those days. "It was his second year of teaching there, and everybody wanted to be in his class, and I felt fortunate to be in there. He was very entertaining as a teacher, but we were learning. Mr. Law was fun, but you knew you had to behave and you had to study. We felt bad when he left Field to go to the North Side, but he still came around and kept up with us and I was part of the groups that went to places like the roller rink, the theater, to his lake place for swimming and boating, and to McDonald's.

"One time, we were having a fashion show at school and he knew I couldn't afford an outfit, so he bought one for me," recalls Richardson, who grew up with four brothers on Clinton Avenue on the South Side, close to Field. "Usually, however, he wasn't just giving things to people. He wanted you to earn it, to work for something so you could buy your own clothes or bikes, or whatever they wanted. It was mostly the boys who sold the candy, however.

"Some kids were jealous of me, even as an adult, because they felt Mr. Law favored me," states Richardson. "Allan has told me that people have asked him who his favorite was and he says it's me. Maybe he says that about others too."

The reserved and sincere Richardson adds, "Many families didn't have a father in their home, so he became like a stepfather to a lot of us. It didn't bother us that he was a white man because he's just a good human being wanting to help others. It didn't matter if you were Black or Native American, you were just a person to him."

The widowed Richardson is retired from her job as a certified nursing assistant. She graduated from Minneapolis Washburn and then attended Hennepin Community College before her thirty-year career in the health care profession. She remarks, "My mom was in charge at our house, and she came to trust him and what he was doing with us kids after school. He had to prove himself as a white man in our Black community. He made sure that everything was aboveboard, and he was always appropriate with us. There was never a reason to question his motives and if something didn't seem right with him, I would have told my mother.

"Mr. Law was a household name in our community and all of the other neighborhoods," comments Frankie. "He's in the poor neighborhoods because they are the people in need. He's not scared of the people he helps. His upbringing had a big effect on him: he experienced good and caring people in his parents and he has lived out what he envisioned his mission in life to be. He truly loves others. Many of us students have children and grandchildren who all know and admire him."

Law is still helping Richardson after all these years. In early 2023, Frankie had her car stolen. After a joyride, it was found. Shortly thereafter, it was stolen again, but this time

*Frankie Richardson, former student and Love
One Another board member.*

it was damaged and needed eight thousand dollars in repairs. Allan helped pay Frankie's deductible and provided bus tokens for her bus transportation for three months while the repair work was done.

"He's just a wonderful person, and I am so glad he has been in my life," says an appreciative Richardson. "His priority is always helping people. He's a little crazy and unpredictable, and he's never usually on time because he operates on his time, not your time. But you can trust he is out there helping someone, somewhere. It's amazing what he does because the average person couldn't keep his hours. I rode with him at night, just once, and I spent most of the time sleeping."

Of course, Richardson sees Law somewhat regularly at their board of directors meetings. Asked about those gatherings, Frankie chuckles and says, "We are not real formal, as we usually meet at Perkins, and it is very comfortable. We are there for about three hours and we talk about following our mission, staying on track with the organization, and dealing with ways to make it better."

Another prominent person in Law's life has been Johnny Hunter, the former director of Hospitality House Youth Development at 1220 North Logan in North Minneapolis, who retired at the end of 2023. Hunter, now sixty-six and a resident of Robbinsdale, was a sixth-grade student of Law's at Willard Elementary in 1969–70.

"That year was one of the best I ever had in school," remarks Hunter, more than fifty years later. "Even though we were learning, it was so fun and very exciting to be there every day. He was just a thrilling teacher and an amazing man; he was a loving person and always urged us to be responsible and respectable. Without question, the best teacher I ever had.

"One time, I was ready to get involved in a fight at recess," remembers Hunter. "He stopped the impending altercation and brought us all into the gym. He gets between the two would-be fighters, and he makes up names for us, like Hurricane Johnny and Power-Fisted Larry, and tells us what great fighters we are and asking the kids who was going to win. Everybody was laughing and this went on for about ten minutes while he was just talking away, but he told us there were better ways to handle our disagreements. We two combatants forgot all about fighting; he diffused a tense situation with ease."

Hunter, one of twenty children in his family, was eleven

years old and living on Morgan Avenue North when Law was commandeering his candy sales crowd one weekend. John vividly recalls, "It was a rainy day that Saturday, and he told me I could take a whole case of candy, fifteen to twenty boxes of taffy, home with me. I didn't think it was all for my family and that I had to bring it back for selling at another time. As it was, all my sisters and brothers and their friends ate it all by Monday morning, and now I was scared that I didn't have any money for all that candy and would have to pay for it all. I didn't know quite what to do, so I told him that the candy had spoiled and I had to throw it away. Well, Mr. Law roars with laughter and to this day jokes about it by saying, 'Oh, Johnny, it all spoiled, huh.' Of course, he just wanted to have our family have the candy for a treat."

Johnny Hunter often saw his former teacher at Hospitality House and on the streets. The amenable Hunter states, "Allan had a lot to do with the kind of work I do, of course. He's been a godsend to North Minneapolis and a blessing to so many families over the years. His passion and dedication to feeding the homeless and helping the poor is truly unbelievable. His spirit of service is so obvious, and he has no hidden agenda; it's just about caring about the people. Allan has donated sandwiches and fed the kids here for many, many years."

Law's lessons have turned into the fruit of Hunter's own impressive humanitarian work. After graduating from Minneapolis North, Johnny matriculated to Anoka-Ramsey Junior College and then Indiana Baptist College and

North Central Bible College. He was pastor for fifteen years at First Community Recovery Church in North Minneapolis and volunteered at various nonprofit organizations and for the Minneapolis Park Board.

After volunteering at Hospitality House for a few years, he joined the board of directors and eventually became the executive director. Johnny says his organization, which receives donations from the community, serves hundreds of kids. He says, "Our mission is to teach kids about Christ and to try and close the achievement gap that has become so glaring." In order to aid his cause and his leadership skills, Hunter has taken fundraising classes at the University of St. Thomas and chemical dependency classes at Metro State University.

"We have an average of about a hundred and fifty kids in our program after school each day," adds Hunter. "Our after-school program has certified teacher help, mostly interns from local colleges and retired teachers. Plus, we have baseball and basketball programs, and our Christmas with Dignity program serves over fifteen hundred kids, thanks to the generosity from the local community."

Jean Allen taught with Law for more than a decade at Andersen. Allen, who got a degree in both art and education from St. Catherine University, has vivid memories of his unconventional methods. After earning her degree in special education at the University of St. Thomas, she served in that capacity at Andersen from 1989 to 2005. During her tenure there, she was one of three special-education teachers who taught in assigned classes. For several years, each of those teachers taught a specific skill, behavior, or concept for that week, such as the importance of sportsmanship or how to deal with anger.

"Allan Law was certainly unorthodox in his teaching methods, but he was one in a million," remembers Allen. "The kids just simply loved him, the parents loved him, and he loved them. He was very involved with them, inside and outside of school, and he did some very unusual things, but they were all about helping them and their families. Allan was so fun-loving and such a prankster.

"One year, I had just finished setting up and decorating my own classroom for the first day of classes on a Friday," recalls Allen, laughing. "When I returned on Monday for the first day of classes, I found a sign taped to the door of the class that said that Mrs. Allen's room has been moved to such and such room. As it turns out, that supposed new room was the boys' bathroom. I had also noticed that a few of my posters were missing from my room and others were askew. So, I entered the boys' lavatory after knocking, and in there I find a small desk and chair and some of my other classroom items. On the wall was one of my posters, 'Peace to the World.' He loved to tease me and that was a memorable one. He always refers to that poster and that occasion when I run into him.

"That man was so generous with his time and with his money," added Allen. "One year, on the last day of school for the sixth-grade graduation, he hired a stretch limousine to pick the kids up and bring them home. That limousine made a lot of trips. Every year for the ceremony, he would provide for a large balloon arch, and it was beautiful."

Allen does see Mr. Law once in a while, including once when a Girl Scout troop she was involved with made sandwiches for his cause. She also attended the initial showing of *The Starfish Throwers* at St. Anthony Main in 2014. Her admiration for her former colleague is readily apparent and she, like most people who have been associated with him, is astonished with what he has done since he retired from the teaching profession. "His passion for wanting to help people is so deep," adds Allen. "To do what he is doing, and at his age, is phenomenal."

A friend of Jean Allen and another teaching colleague of Allan Law was Vicki Sommers, a Minneapolis resident who now works as a realtor for Edina Realty. After being educated at St. Cloud State and the University of Minnesota, Sommers spent thirty-two years working in the Minneapolis school system at the elementary and district level. She taught fourth grade at Andersen for ten years, starting in the early 1980s. It was there that Sommers became associated with Law.

"The kids loved him as a teacher because he was very laid-back," remarks Sommers. "Certainly, he had an entirely different approach to teaching than most others. He had a couch in his room, and he would listen to the kids, and they respected that and so they behaved well for him.

"Allan was a real character, of course, and everyone knew him because he was always teasing and joking around," continues Sommers. "He always had something to say and could talk about any subject or topic. He was usually up to something in the teachers' lounge. I have to giggle when I think of him because I could smell him from a distance away because he wore some pretty heavy cologne in those days."

Sommers, who also taught at Whittier Elementary and the Laura Ingalls Wilder School, among others, is so appreciative of his efforts with the underprivileged children and the homeless in the area. "It is amazing what he has done with his life, serving people," adds Vicki. "We saw it in his teaching, that he truly cared for people. I still see him around the city: at the gas station, on the road with his van, and even when he comes to our realty office when we have made sandwiches for him."

All told, Mr. Law taught four years of fifth grade and twenty-eight years of sixth grade before retiring in the spring of 1999.

Chapter Nine

THE STARFISH THROWERS

In 2010, budding filmmaker Jesse Roesler came across an article by Jim Walsh that portrayed the life of a man who fed and clothed the poor, and it intrigued him. That man, of course, was one Allan Law, the so-called Sandwich Man. Roesler, who grew up in central Wisconsin, had graduated from the University of Minnesota with a degree in journalism in 2004 and had spent his early employment years in the communications field in the Twin Cities.

However, his first exposure to Law came when the Minneapolis resident saw Allan's black van with white trim sporting about the downtown streets. The amiable Roesler says, "I had witnessed this van before and had wondered about the program, and after reading the article, the next time I saw his vehicle, I jotted down the phone number of his organization written on the side, and that's how I actually got access to him."

A passionate fan of food and cooking, Roesler developed the idea to do a film about people feeding the poor. It seemed like a natural fit. He says, "At first, the film was just going to focus on what Allan was doing, but after doing more research into the subject, I decided to also add two more individuals and feature their unique and heroic efforts in helping others."

Jesse Roesler, director of The Starfish Throwers. *(Courtesy of Jesse Roesler)*

Roesler says it took just old-fashioned journalistic research to find ten to fifteen more people who were fighting the hunger issue who might meld into the two segments opposite Allan's part. "I did a deeper dive into all of those others to determine who might fill the bill for the other two subjects," says the U of M alum. "Finally, it just seemed right to target Katie Stagliano and Narayanan Krishnan, and with the three of them, I felt it was a good balance: a retired teacher working throughout the night in the Midwest; a former chef feeding and caring for the poor in Madurai, India; and a twelve-year-old girl in South Carolina who develops gardens to feed the poor.

"It took me six months to convince Allan to do this project," says Roesler. "I had asked him at least a dozen times but he said he was either too busy or it was too dangerous out on the streets. Finally, I was able to convey to him

The Starfish Throwers *DVD cover jacket. (Courtesy of Jesse Roesler)*

that this film was not just about him but about how others could be inspired to do good, and he ultimately agreed." Sure enough, filming for the three segments commenced in late 2011 and wrapped up early in 2013. Roesler, who was the director and producer of the film, also did almost all of the actual filming, and his work is exemplary. Counting sit-down interviews and ride-alongs, Roesler rolled up nearly twenty-five hours of film for the Law portion alone.

Untold hours of film were also captured in India and in Summerville, South Carolina. Roesler figures he spent two weeks in India on his first foray there and another week on his second trip to Asia. His destination, Madurai, is a city of a million residents in the southern part of the country with a documented history of over 2,500 years. As for South Carolina, he ventured to the Palmetto State three or four times, with each trip lasting three or four days to Summerville, a suburb of fifty thousand near Charleston.

"As for Allan, he puts people at ease," recalls Roesler, who is back living in Chetek in his native state with his wife, Jen, and their two boys. "Mr. Law has a way of connecting quickly with people that is truly unique. He really cares about people and his compassion is quite evident. Allan asks questions and he listens, and he can remember something about them when he sees them again, and that creates a deep bond between those he serves."

Roesler continues, "I think about him often and admire how he is so curious in inquiring about the people he deals with, but he never judges them and that is a great quality to possess." Roesler got an up-close view of Law's nightly sojourns searching for people to help and also on his daily trips to schools, churches, and other organizations, gathering up supplies for that evening's deliveries or restocking them into his rental spaces.

"It was just amazing to see what he does, day after day, night after night," remarks Jesse, ten years after the release of *The Starfish Throwers*. Two scenes stand out for him in witnessing and filming this incredible show of humanity. Roesler says, "One is the first time I saw all those freezers in his condo with all the sandwiches inside; it is something to hear about but another to really see it with your own eyes.

"The second is when we got wind through his assistant Steven Aase that he might be leaving the rehab center he was in after undergoing cancer surgery in 2013," remarks Jesse. "It was very late at night, and I came over to the center, and we got film of him leaving. It was a moment to never forget. He didn't care about his health condition; he wanted to go out there to see who he could help. It was a perfect example of his character and his motivation. The staff there certainly wasn't happy about it, but he did it a few more times before he left for good."

The Starfish Throwers was released on March 16, 2014, and received great fanfare. Editor Bill Kersey spent several months editing after the filming was complete, and then Melody Gilbert was key in the distribution process. "I had a feeling it was going to be a good product while I was filming," recalls Roesler. "The stories of each of the subjects really moved me, and so I had a hunch it would be a hit. But it was my first film, so I couldn't be sure of its impact."

The feature-length film is eighty-three minutes long and was named "The Most Heartwarming Film of the Year" for 2014 by the *Huffington Post*. Roesler, who has gone on to win an Emmy and a James Beard award for his work, utilizes a unique narrative for his films. He explains, "We script our documentaries but use something called 'scripted/un-

A recuperating Law leaves a rehab center without permission late at night to serve the homeless. (Courtesy of Jesse Roesler)

scripted' since we work a lot with real people. We draft storylines that contain key messages and structure, but then we draft questions that allow our subjects, such as Allan, to answer questions in their own words for maximum authenticity."

The first-person narrative displayed in the film definitely developed the true character of Mr. Law, his unpretentiousness, and his authentic love for the less fortunate. Roesler shows his cinematic gifts by unearthing Allan's concern for those he serves with several unforgettable lines. This type of filmography puts the power of visual storytelling to work for global brands and causes, such as the efforts to curb hunger displayed in *The Starfish Throwers*.

Roesler believes that storytelling has the power to inspire immense positive change; he also speaks frequently on this topic via keynotes and leadership workshops to large national corporations, such as Best Buy and United Way. His work for clients like Starbucks, Feeding America, Food Network, and the *New York Times* have garnered more than twenty-five million views online.

In the film, Roesler's camera captures a myriad of typical scenes repeated by the Sandwich Man day after day, night after night. Allan is shown driving amidst the inner-city streets in search of the homeless and destitute; collecting sandwiches made by a school group, church group, or company; visiting one of his storage areas to gather clothing and personal items for dispersal; transporting bins of food and clothing; making jokes with the homeless while handing out sandwiches; and even trying to catch a wink of sleep in some deserted parking lot.

One of the most interesting scenes depicts Allan Law in his condominium, tossing frozen sandwiches from one of his seventeen freezers onto the floor so that they can be thawed in time for distribution later that evening. It appears that the entire carpeted surface is strewn with the sandwiches, most with cheese and bologna inside. He calmly places them in grocery carts and heads down the hall, down the elevator, and eventually to his waiting Ford van. Law tells the viewers that each freezer holds up to a thousand sandwiches and that he has a regular rotation in order for him to utilize the sandwiches within a month's time.

Throughout the film, he utters his standard, "How you doing today?" numerous times as he greets those he approaches, with an emphasis on the "you." Among his most noteworthy comments are:

- "If I won the lottery, I would still be out on the streets."
- "I have to be out every night; no exceptions."
- "This is my life. It's not a job."
- "I don't have time to worry about my safety, illness, or injuries."
- "This is what I have to do for the rest of my life."
- "People can tell if you really do care."
- "The gangs don't bother me because they know what I do."
- "Every night, I meet people who truly do need my help."
- "I'm on call twenty-four hours a day; the homeless know they can count on me."
- "My number-one mission is compassion."

Roesler's first film is poignant, touching, and stimulating. It intimately explores how three of the world's most fiercely compassionate individuals fight hunger in their unique struggles to restore hope to the hopeless. All three exhibit incredible energy and determination. Roesler enhances this modeling as a blueprint for how one solitary person can motivate others to make a difference. Instead of simply dividing each story as a separate segment, the director repeatedly intersperses video from each story with one of the other's audio clips, and it comes off brilliantly.

There is no way to determine what motivating effect the film has had on others to volunteer in whatever way they can; however, one can imagine it has been immense. Perhaps few people in the world can mirror what Allan, Katie,

Law and Katie Stagliano at the debut of The Starfish Throwers *at St. Anthony Main in 2014. (Courtesy of Jesse Roesler)*

and Narayanan have accomplished, but their contributions are stupendous and worthy of lofty recognition and praise. One person at a time, giving selflessly, can change the world, helping one person at a time while inspiring others to act in their own specific manner. Few, if any, can replicate what this seventy-nine-year-old former teacher, five-star chef, or twelve-year-old girl have done, but we can all do something.

The name of the film was inspired by a story written by Loren Eiseley called "The Star Thrower." The following is an adaption of that tale:

> *It all started when a young girl was walking along a beach upon which thousands of starfish had washed up during a terrible storm. When she came up to each starfish, she would pick it up*

*and throw it back into the ocean. People watched
her with amusement.*

*She had been doing this for some time when an
old man approached her and said, "Little girl,
why are you doing this? Look at this beach! You
can't save all these starfish. You can't begin to
make a difference!" The girl seemed crushed,
suddenly deflated. But after a few moments, she
bent down, picked up another starfish, and hurled
it as far as she could into the ocean. Then she
looked up at the man and replied, "Well, I made
a difference for that one." The man looked at the
girl inquisitively and thought about what she
had done and said. Inspired, he joined the little
girl in throwing starfish back into the sea. Soon
others joined, and all the starfish were saved.*

Perhaps the main point of *The Starfish Throwers* is that if
you truly care about humanity and the human condition,
you should simply act to help out in the community. No
matter how small the time commitment or the sacrifice, just
help. A sincere heart can do wonders, one filled with love,
hope, and charity. Just because a single action is small, it
doesn't mean it isn't worthwhile. It reminds us when the
world's problems seem insurmountable, our efforts can
mean everything to someone.

The film is used as a promotional tool by Love One Another and is shown to many of the volunteer groups prior to

their sandwich-making events. It has created a great desire for people to help in other capacities besides the world of hunger. The goal, of course, is to inspire one to help others. Educational materials have been created to go with the film in Canada, and after the initial film festival tour, Love One Another started getting emails and letters from all over the world.

Years later, Jesse Roesler's admiration for Allan Law remains strong, and he contemplates his life frequently. "The man's compassion for people is real and genuine, and he is a walking image of empathy for others," states Jesse. "This world can certainly use a lot more people like him, no doubt. You don't have to hand out a thousand sandwiches a night like him in order to create a ripple effect that can last for many years. Allan truly cares and he has left a great legacy in inspiring others."

Stagliano became the founder of Katie's Krops, a nonprofit organization with a mission of empowering youth to start and maintain vegetable gardens of all sizes for donation of the harvest to help people with hunger. As a third-grader, Katie had grown a forty-pound cabbage and donated it to a local soup kitchen that fed 275 people. The next year, her fourth-grade class grew their own garden, and a movement had begun. Currently, there are more than one hundred youth-based gardens in over thirty states. In 2012, at twelve years old, she became the youngest recipient of the Clinton Global Citizen Award and is also the author of a winning children's book entitled *Katie's Cabbage*.

Quoted in the documentary, Katie states, "I can't end

Katie Stagliano (right) and her mother, Stacy, harvest lettuce outside their home in Summerville, South Carolina. (Courtesy of Jesse Roesler)

hunger by myself, but you may never know what one small action can do to inspire people to help; you can make a difference."

Meanwhile, Narayanan Krishnan gave up his job as a five-star hotel chef in 2002 to devote himself full-time to feeding and clothing the poor. His organization, Akshaya Trust, is similar to Law's Love One Another in that it gives no salaries to any of its volunteers. Krishnan feeds at least 425 people three meals each day in addition to also bathing and barbering others when he finds the destitute on the streets. A devout Hindu, Narayanan came from Brahmin, a caste considered to be the highest in the system. The Brahmin are pure vegetarians and are forbidden to touch or mingle with people of lower communities. Narayanan, however, feels his destiny is to serve God and humanity through his service.

Narayanan Krishnan feeds a homeless person in
Madurai, India. (Courtesy of Jesse Roesler)

"All humans have dignity, and my mission is to feed, clothe, and bathe people," remarks Krishnan in the film. "I put physical ingredients in the food I prepare but I also put in the spiritual ingredient, love, also." He was selected as one of the top ten in the 2010 CNN Heroes list, which honors everyday people who are changing the world. Narayanan started the Akshaya Home for the homeless in 2013.

Chapter Ten

AWARDS AND RECOGNITION

Over the years, Love One Another and founder/ executive director Allan Law have been fortunate to receive extraordinary and expansive media coverage for their efforts in serving the homeless community. Besides a look at their unique history, the attention has given much exposure to their volunteers and donors.

Following is a partial list of awards and recognition garnered by Allan Law and his organization:

- American Institute for Public Service: Jacqueline Kennedy Onassis Gold Award for Outstanding Public Service Benefitting Local Communities (presented at the United States Supreme Court)
- American Institute for Public Service: National Jefferson Award (presented at the United States Senate)
- Recognition from President George W. Bush
- Recognition from President Bill Clinton
- Recognition from President George H. W. Bush
- Recognition in the US Congressional Record by Minnesota Senator Paul Wellstone
- Recognition from Minnesota Senators Rod Grams and Mark Dayton

Sen. John Glenn from Ohio presents Law with the Gold Medallion as part of the Jefferson Awards for Public Service in 2000 in Washington, DC. (Courtesy of the Law family)

- Recognition from Minnesota Congressman Jim Ramstad
- Recognition from Minnesota Governors Tim Pawlenty and Jesse Ventura
- Recognition from Minnesota Attorney General Mike Hatch
- Recognition from Minneapolis Mayor Sharon Sayles Belton: The Minneapolis Award
- Recognition from the McKnight Foundation: Virginia McKnight Binger Award in Human Service
- City of Minneapolis: Martin Luther King Award
- Points of Light Foundation: Daily Point of Light Award
- Salvation Army: Outstanding Volunteer Service Award

Allan Law offers a toy puppy to a toddler at the Salvation Army in Minneapolis. (Courtesy of Jesse Roesler)

- Minnehaha Academy: Alumnus of the Year Award
- City Business Magazine: 100 Unsung Heroes Award
- Catholic Charities: Volunteer Service Award
- North Minneapolis: Community Service Award
- KARE 11 TV: Eleven Who Care Award
- WCCO TV: Hometown Hero Award
- Recognition from Kiwanis, Optimist, and Rotary Clubs
- Ventura for Minnesota: Public Service Award
- WCCO Radio: Good Neighbor Award
- Minnehaha Academy: Centennial Award—100 Alumni Who Have Influenced Our World
- City of Edina: 2014 Hometown Hero Award
- Rotary Club of Minneapolis: 2015 Service Above Self Award

The Law family celebrates Allan's recognition at the KARE 11 Gala in 1999. (Courtesy of the Law family)

- Salvation Army: 2015 Harbor Light Center Master and Commander Award
- Featured in the 2014 Documentary Film, *The Starfish Throwers*
- Featured in 2015 Book, *Unselfish: Love Thy Neighbor As Thy Selfie*

In addition, innumerable articles have been written and videos filmed concerning Law and Love One Another. Below is a partial list of media outlets that can be accessed for information.

- Nation Swell: "The Sandwich Man"
- NBC Nightly News: "Sandwich Man Delivers Helping of Hope to the Hungry"

The Sandwich Man visits with a man in a wheelchair on a cold winter night. (Courtesy of Jesse Roesler)

- *Huffington Post*: "Minneapolis Man Handed Out 520,000 Sandwiches to Homeless in a Year. That's Minnesota Nice."
- Nation Swell: "Allan Law distributes sandwiches from mini-van that displays the words Love One Another"
- Get Inspired: "Meet the Sandwich Man"
- Examiner.com: "*The Starfish Throwers* shows the power of one on a global scale"
- The City of Edina: "Meet Edina Hometown Hero"
- Upworthy: "This Goes Out to Everyone Who . . ."
- Documentary Film: *The Starfish Throwers*
- *Star Tribune*: "Local filmmaker tackles hunger one small act at a time"
- The Minnesota Egoist: "MPLS Filmmaker Found Real 'Starfish Throwers'"
- KMSP TV Fox 9 News: "Sandwiches and Starfish"

- *Star Tribune*: "Sandwiches from a Savior"
- *TC Daily Planet*: "Sandwich Man serves food to inner-city homeless 363 days"
- KARE 11 TV: "Eleven Who Care Winner: Allan Law"
- *Sun Press and News*: "OMG Legion family makes 970 sandwiches for 363 Food Program"
- *Star Tribune*: "'Retired' teacher with a van just keeps educating kids"

AFTERWORD

My buddy Bruce Hendrickson was right when he told me that I was about to meet the most amazing person I would ever meet back in April 2017. After that initial chance encounter with the enigmatic Allan Law at McDonald's, it has been my distinct pleasure to work on this book to give recognition and honor to a truly remarkable man. Indeed, it has been a long but enlightening road. Allan is a fascinating character and a real original, always entertaining, outspoken, and lighthearted. What he has wrought is truly astounding on both a physical and emotional level.

Allan's dedication and sacrifice know no bounds. He literally gives all of his energy and will to help others, and his powerful impact on the Twin Cities scene is undeniable. Not only has he provided the basic necessities for those in need, but his dynamic personality has also brought joy, humor, compassion, and hope to those he serves.

To the people associated with Love One Another, Minneapolis Recreation Development, and the extended Law family, my appreciation and gratitude are endless. As for Allan Law, the words I have used to describe him somehow seem inadequate. I have nothing but profound respect and admiration for what he has accomplished and for what he continues to do, every night and every day. He's an authentic hero right here in our midst.

I am humbled and honored to have had the opportunity to complete this book and sincerely hope that others may, in whatever fashion, emulate the selfless service inspired by founder and executive director Allan Law and his Love One Another organization.

"A GOD SERVANT FATHER"

God gives us many gifts
But far above any other
He gave us a Christian father
Mr. Law, without you in our lives
We may not still be alive
You have fed us
Clothed us
Counseled with us
Been there for us
You have taught us the right way to live
To think and to love
We love you and we thank you
For that we will never forget you
Words cannot tell you how we love you
God sent us an angel
And his name is Mr. Law

—From Your Northside Family

DONATIONS

To help serve the growing number in our community in urgent need, please consider partnering with Love One Another by making a tax-deductible donation. Donations can be made on the website (www.mrdinc.org), or by mail to:

Minneapolis Recreation Development

7220 York Avenue South, #602

Edina, MN 55435

Contact: Allan Law, Founder and Executive Director

Phone: (612) 423-9923

Email: mrd.363days@gmail.com

Website: www.mrdinc.org

Facebook: www.facebook.com/mr.allanlaw

Member MN Council of Nonprofits

Federal 501(c)(3) EIN: 41-1836443

To volunteer to make sandwiches, please fill out the request form on the website (www.mrdinc.org). Once your request is received, your name or group name will be placed on the calendar, and you will receive an email confirmation. Sandwich-making instructions along with answers to frequently asked questions are also provided on the website. If you have additional questions, contact Allan Law (612) 423-9923. Thank you!

ACKNOWLEDGMENTS

I would like to thank all of the people who supported my efforts in compiling this book and those who gave me suggestions and counsel, especially my good friends Tom Novitzki, Bruce Hendrickson, Bill Marshall, and Linda Storlie. For those unnamed collaborators, my sincere appreciation for your willingness to share your ideas and thoughts in order to make this project a success.

Thanks again to my publisher, Lily Coyle at Beaver's Pond Press, for her assistance in working on this book together and for her trust in my work and the worthiness of this endeavor. A special thank you to Laurie Buss Herrmann for her exemplary work on book organization, layout, and editing of this publication. Well-deserved kudos to my friend Paul Roff, whose artistic skill is exhibited on the front and back covers, our fifth working together. And to my wife, Ann, for her undying support for my writing ventures and for her spot-on observations.

Photographs courtesy of the author, Allan Law, the Law family, Jesse Roesler, Love One Another, and Minneapolis Recreation Development.

JIM HOEY was born and raised in Taconite, Minnesota, and graduated from Greenway High School in Coleraine and from Saint Mary's University in Winona. He spent thirty-four years as a secondary school social studies teacher in Shakopee and Farmington, mainly as an instructor in American history, political science, and geography. He also served as head boys' hockey coach at both high schools. The Iron Range native was also a sportswriter for the *Rosemount Town Pages* and the *Farmington Independent*.

Hoey published his first book, *Minnesota Twins Trivia*, in 2010. Subsequent books published include *Puck Heaven* (2011), on the Minnesota State Boys Hockey Tournament; *Minnesota Vikings Trivia* (2013); *Ike: Minnesota Hockey Icon* (2015) with former Edina coach Willard Ikola; and *Honoring Those Who Honor* (2017), about the Memorial Rifle Squad at Fort Snelling National Cemetery. Each of those books was published by Nodin Press. Hoey lives in Eagan with his wife, Ann.